Preparing for Graduate School Academic Writing

Ashan R. Hampton

Cornerstone Publishing

Arkansas

Published by Cornerstone Communications & Publishing, Little Rock, Arkansas.

Cover Design: Ashan R. Hampton
Cover Photo: © *Can Stock Photo / klyaksun*
Interior Photos: Pexels | CanStock | Unsplash.com

Websites: www.arhampton.com
www.prowritingskills.com

Library of Congress Control Number: 2020909763
ISBN: 978-1-71689-000-0

Printed in the United States of America.

First Edition.

Cataloging-in-Publication Data is on file with the Library of Congress.

10 9 8 7 6 5 4 3 2 1

PRO Writing Skills
Online Classes

- Beyond Basic Grammar
- Business Grammar Essentials
- Core Grammar Essentials
- Graduate Research Writing
- Grant Writing Essentials
- Proofreading Power
- Public Speaking Skills & Drills
- Smarty Pants Vocabulary Builders
- Workplace Grammar & Style

www.arhampton.com/classes
www.prowritingskills.com

About the Author

Ashan R. Hampton has worked as an English instructor in higher education for over 20 years, most notably at Morehouse College in Atlanta, Georgia. She is also a proud graduate of the *Donaghey Scholars Program* at the University of Arkansas at Little Rock under the direction of Dr. C. Earl Ramsey, Emeritus.

Ashan's original research, *History of the Arkansas State Hospital 1859-1930*, was published in the *Pulaski County Historical Review* (1995) and continues to be cited by history scholars today. Her articles on notable African American Arkansans also appear in the *Encyclopedia of Arkansas History and Culture*.

With her doctoral studies on hold, Ashan has found success in online education. She produces and teaches her own writing and grammar courses for global audiences through her company, Cornerstone Communications & Publishing. Ashan is also a published author, digital media producer, proofreader and copyeditor.

Visit her website: **www.arhampton.com**.

Contents

Introduction

Graduate school is all about writing. Are you prepared to write 15-20-page academic papers? How about 200+ pages of a thesis or a dissertation? Do you know how to take a blank page and create a scholarly research project? Most graduate programs do not offer a course that prepares you for this level of professional writing. However, without strong writing skills, you will not succeed in your master's or doctoral program.

"Preparing for Graduate School Academic Writing" assesses your readiness for graduate learning through surveys, exercises, and succinct introductory lessons on the most essential aspects of graduate writing, such as standards, style, plagiarism, source evaluation, and digital library research skills.

As a potential, current or returning graduate student, you must become familiar with peer-reviewed articles, literature reviews, abstracts, references, and annotated bibliographies before advancing too far into your program of study. Otherwise, you might get overwhelmed by the expectations to immediately produce this kind of content with very little instruction. Therefore, equipping yourself for the rigors of academic writing is worth the extra time and effort to avoid stress, confusion or burnout.

The difference between undergraduate and graduate-level writing is the difference between student and scholar. As a graduate-level writer, you engage other scholars as peers, building on and challenging their ideas to advance your area of research. What does that mean exactly? For example, I actually engaged in graduate level writing as an undergraduate. In order to graduate from the honors program, I needed to write a senior thesis on any topic that received the blessings of my committee. I researched the growth of mental illness facilities within my state. As it turns out, no one had ever done that before.

For one year, I researched and wrote from primary sources like old newspaper articles from the 1800s preserved on microfiche. I interviewed older people with memories to share about my topic. I typed my project on an old *Brother* word processor and saved it to a floppy disk. Yes, definitely old school! What emerged from all of that hard work was "The History of the Arkansas State Hospital 1859-1930," which won a local history award, and was published in the *Pulaski County Historical Review* in 1995. Still today, other researchers and state historians who write on this topic quote my work. In this instance, I moved from being a consumer to a producer of knowledge that turned into a published, peer-reviewed article. Since there were no other sources from other scholars that I could include in my work, I became the source. Similarly, you must find an area of research within your discipline that lacks a particular perspective that you will offer through researching and writing your thesis or dissertation. Instead of creating original research, you will shed light on established ideas, analyze the assumptions of another person's work, and contribute your own thoughts about a topic. In a nutshell, this is the crux of graduate level writing.

You might be thinking, *I don't want to be a celebrated scholar. I just want to pass my classes so that I can get my degree.* Of course. To that end, this book will walk you through typical graduate student activities like writing discussion posts, papers, and conducting online research while providing show-and-tell examples for fast and easy comprehension.

Along the way, you will have opportunities to assess your current academic skills and identify strengths and weaknesses to improve upon before diving into your program of study. Doing so will boost your confidence in completing complex writing assignments before tackling a full master's or dissertation proposal. Remember, writing is the primary basis for assessment in graduate school, not quizzes or tests. Therefore, you must actively increase your academic writing abilities to ensure success in your classes.

Some of you reading this book might be brand new to graduate learning, returning from a long break, or transitioning directly from an undergraduate program. No matter your starting point or previous academic experience, the information in the chapters that follow are an asset to anyone brave enough to pursue the highest levels of educational achievement.

Chapter One
Graduate School Readiness

Photo by Fizkes from Can Stock Photo.

Are You Ready for Graduate School?

Regardless of what type of graduate school you enroll in, some things are common to the lives of all graduate students. Number one, you will write...a lot! Number two, you will read...a lot! Whether online or in person, reading and writing complex materials are required activities for all graduate level classes. You will also create discussion posts, send plenty of emails to instructors and fellow students, as well as submit long and short research papers.

If you do not adopt a proper growth mindset and organization strategies before entering graduate school, you will faint at the amount of work you must accomplish in a short amount of time. There are plenty of drop-outs around to prove that this is more than a theory. Have you ever met anyone who didn't quite finish their master's or doctoral degrees? Of course, you have.

So, to avoid this fate, ask yourself some questions to really gauge your skill levels and attitudes about the task you are getting ready to undertake. The following survey questions prompt you to think about your writing and research skills in addition to your readiness to join a new academic community. Use the space provided to note any information you might need to learn or update prior to your first class.

Writing Skills Survey

Consider your prior or current writing experiences when answering these questions. Use the space provided at the end of the survey to note any unfamiliar terms that appear within the questions.

In the past, I have written:

1. An academic paper that is at least 10 pages long.
   - yes
   - no

2. An academic paper that is 15-20 pages long.
   - yes
   - no

3. An academic paper using APA style.
   - yes
   - no

4. An academic paper using MLA or another academic style.
   - yes
   - no

5. An annotated bibliography with at least 10 sources.
   - yes
   - no

6. A literature review.
   - yes
   - no

7. A conference paper or a published academic article.
   - yes
   - no

8. I have written more than one paper at the last minute.
   - yes
   - no

9. In the past, I have typically read____pages a week for each of my classes.
    - 5-15 pages
    - 20 or more pages
    - More than 50 pages

10. When it comes to grammar, spelling and language usage, I rate my skill level as:
    - above average
    - average
    - proficient
    - needing improvement

11. I typically meet the deadlines for my writing assignments:
    - all of the time
    - most of the time
    - not at all

12. When writing an academic paper, I usually ask for feedback from:
    - instructors
    - tutors
    - classmates
    - no one

13. In the past, I have included my own analysis in academic papers.
    - frequently
    - sometimes
    - not at all

14. When writing an academic paper, I usually:
    - write and revise one draft
    - write and revise multiple drafts
    - write and submit with very little revision

15. When writing an academic paper, I usually:
    - create an outline before starting
    - create an outline as I write
    - write without an outline

16. When reading something I plan to include in a paper, I usually:
- take notes without highlighting/underlining
- take notes in addition to highlighting/underlining
- just read without taking notes or highlighting

17. I am comfortable writing a thesis statement.
- yes
- no

18. I am comfortable writing a bibliography or reference page.
- yes
- no

19. I am comfortable using direct quotes or paraphrases.
- yes
- no

20. I am comfortable writing signal phrases within paragraphs.
- yes
- no

21. I know how to use evidence to support the main ideas in my paper.
- yes
- no

22. I am comfortable incorporating evidence and analysis in my papers.
- yes
- no

23. It is acceptable to include more than one idea in a paragraph.
- yes
- no

24. Sometimes it is difficult for me to get my ideas down on paper.
- yes
- no

25. When I sit down to write, I know how to effectively organize my papers.
- yes
- no

My Notes

Helpful Writing Resources

B & W Print
ISBN: 978-1-387-91413-5

Grammar Essentials for Proofreading, Copyediting & Business Writing focuses on the grammar and usage topics you need to improve your writing skills for personal and professional success. Learn how to correct common grammar errors like fragments, run-ons, and comma splices while answering usage concerns such as when to use "who" or "whom." Each chapter ends with practical, self-grading exercises.

Ordering information:

www.arhampton.com/books
www.lulu.com

B & W Print
ISBN: 978-0-359-69282-8

"Adult Learner Grammar Essentials" teaches you to effectively correct the most common grammar errors encountered in academic and professional writing. With self-study quizzes, plain English explanations and real-world examples, you will improve your grammar skills in just minutes a day.

Ordering information:

www.arhampton.com/books
www.lulu.com

Research Skills Survey

Although physical libraries still exist, you will conduct most of your research through online databases and libraries. Even if you attend classes in person, you will still be required to incorporate online sources in your assignments. Answer the questions honestly, and note any questions you might have about some of the research concepts mentioned in this survey.

1. Have you ever used an online academic library for research?
    a. yes
    b. no

2. Can you describe the kinds of sources found in an online library?
    a. yes
    b. no

3. Do you have any experience with online library databases that are not freely available on the internet?
    a. yes
    b. no

4. Do you know how to define a topic for a graduate research paper?
    a. yes
    b. no

5. Do you know how to generate key words for a topic search?
    a. yes
    b. no

6. Do you know how to narrow or broaden the scope of your topic?
    a. yes
    b. no

7. Do you know how to effectively use a single-box database search?
    a. yes
    b. no

8. Do you know how to create a Boolean search with the modifiers *"and, not, or"?*
    a. yes
    b. no

9. Can you describe how to evaluate the academic credibility of a source?
    a. yes
    b. no

10. Do you know how to decide if a source is relevant to your topic?
    a. yes
    b. no

11. Do you know how to identify personal or philosophical bias in a source?
    a. yes
    b. no

12. Do you know how to summarize, paraphrase or quote somebody else's writing?
    a. yes
    b. no

13. I approach different types of reading in different ways, including the order in which I read aspects of the text.
    - Not at all
    - Somewhat
    - Very

14. I usually pay attention to the intended audience and the writer's purpose when I read.
    - Not at all
    - Somewhat
    - Very

My Notes

Academic Community Survey

What does it mean to become part of an academic community? As a graduate student, you will join classes with other learners and instructors online or in person. As with any other social group, you are expected to behave respectfully and appropriately in all verbal and written communications.

1. I understand what it means to be part of an academic community.
   - a. yes
   - b. somewhat
   - c. no

2. I understand how I can benefit from an academic community.
   - a. yes
   - b. somewhat
   - c. no

3. I always treat faculty members and fellow learners with respect.
   - a. yes
   - b. somewhat
   - c. no

4. I respond respectfully to people when they disagree with me.
   - a. yes
   - b. somewhat
   - c. no

5. I am respectful of diverse perspectives.
   - a. yes
   - b. somewhat
   - c. no

6. I feel uncomfortable when I encounter opinions and perspectives that are different from my own.
   - a. yes
   - b. somewhat
   - c. no

7. I feel comfortable receiving constructive feedback from others, even if I don't agree with the remarks.
   a. yes
   b. somewhat
   c. no

8. I feel comfortable giving constructive feedback to others, even if it is negative.
   a. yes
   b. somewhat
   c. no

9. I feel comfortable collaborating with faculty members and peers.
   a. yes
   b. somewhat
   c. no

10. I would be willing to write a paper for a classmate in need.
    a. yes
    b. somewhat
    c. no

11. I understand what counts as plagiarism and what does not.
    a. yes
    b. somewhat
    c. no

12. Writing a paper for another student is academically dishonest.
    a. yes
    b. somewhat
    c. no

My Notes

Chapter Two
Academic Writing

Photo from Pexels.

Understanding Academic Writing

Graduate-level writing depends on arguments, and arguments require evidence. While the specific requirements for evidence vary from discipline to discipline and even from project to project (i.e., certain arguments may only require textual evidence from a specific document instead of results from a randomized controlled trial), your writing will usually need support from something other than personal experience.

As a scholar, you will need to evaluate the work of others. This means not only evaluating what was said, but how, when, where, and why it was said. Do not take the sources you find at face value. Just because it is in print, does not mean it is beyond critique. Therefore, recognizing bias and critical thinking errors in published works is essential to forming and supporting your own ideas about a topic.

In addition to developing arguments and evaluating sources, synthesizing academic materials means more than summarizing them. When you synthesize sources, you connect them with your own ideas, and incorporate the subsequent analysis of both into the body of your argument. Instead of just skimming sources for quotes to insert into your paper, approach sources as a whole by engaging with their ideas and supportive evidence. In some disciplines, direct quotes from sources are discouraged, unless the verbatim language of the source is particularly relevant. Basically, at this stage, you will be required to mix your own ideas about a topic with what has already been published to offer new insights, especially if you are writing a dissertation. Let's use an example to put this all together.

Graduate Writing Scenario

Suppose you are a K-12 teacher with an interest in distance learning, which is a hugely broad topic. However, in the education community, lots of opinions are being tossed around and getting published in popular educational journals. When you begin to read some of these articles, you discover that no one really talks about the challenges that teachers and students in low performing schools face with distance learning.

Additionally, not much has been written about minority students and distance learning. Based on your own personal experiences in the classroom, you understand that many of the fancy-pants learning theories on distance education cannot be effectively applied with the student population at your school and more specifically in your classroom. Why? What kinds of students do you have? What kinds of distance learning activities can you use with these students, if any? What are the obstacles you face?

With the published research articles you have read, your personal experience, and the gaps in the literature that you have identified, you have now created a line of research on distance education among impoverished, minority students in K-12 classrooms. You can adjust the scope of your topic as you continue to research by making it more narrow. For example, perhaps you want to focus solely on African American students in high school regarding distance education.

Whenever you write papers on your topic, you are offering a perspective that not many have considered. If you were to get your papers published in a journal, you would be joining a community of educational scholars who are having a conversation about distance learning that you can now contribute to in a fresh and thoughtful way. So, for your class assignments, you should write on your topic as often as possible, because these smaller papers will culminate into your thesis or dissertation research. This is the bottom-line progression of graduate level writing. You're welcome.

Your Writing Experience

How long has it been since you have written an essay or a research paper? Perhaps you have just completed an undergraduate degree and wrote a fair amount of papers along the way. If that is the case, great. You have academic writing tools to build upon. However, if you have been out of the classroom for a few years, writing at this level might seem daunting. Terrifying, even. However, the more you write and the more you receive constructive feedback on your work, you are bound to become a more confident academic writer.

What is Academic Writing?

Academic writing is usually read by students, faculty, researchers, and other professionals in scholarly fields who have need of objective, scientific, and reputable information about subject matter that mainly appeals to higher education audiences. Written in a tone that is formal, concise and unbiased, academic writing seeks to illuminate or challenge existing theories by offering new perspectives or alternative explanations.

In other cases, academic writing promotes brand new empirical research that needs to be vetted by peers in a particular field of study. As a graduate student, your writing will take the form of research papers, proposals, theses, and dissertations that are logically supported by verifiable references from academic literature that is formatted according to your department's style guide of choice, such as APA or MLA.

Types of Academic Writing

In graduate school, you will encounter four academic writing techniques that are often used to compose written assignments. Instead of focusing on just one, forming a solid argument will most likely require a combination of all four, depending on your research topic.

1. Descriptive
2. Analytical
3. Persuasive
4. Critical

Descriptive Writing

Description tells what something—(a person, place, or thing)—looks like, feels like, sounds like, smells like, or tastes like. Descriptive writing relies on the five senses to create visual images for the reader. Just as a reminder, the five senses include: sight, hearing, taste, touch, and smell. Basically, description uses colorful language to highlight nouns, and uses the five senses to create visual images for the reader.

Analytical Writing

Analytical writing involves articulating and supporting complex ideas by constructing and evaluating arguments with a sustained focus on the issue or topic that you are investigating through your research.

The analysis involves using evidence to demonstrate relationships between two or more pieces of information by comparing and contrasting them according to logical soundness, approach, theory, or perspective.

Persuasive Writing

The persuasion or argument technique is used to convince an audience to accept a particular point of view or to perform a particular action. A document that incorporates argument takes a position on an issue and uses valid reasoning that is supported by sufficient evidence. Persuasive writing clearly and logically supports your position with a combination of facts, expert opinions, and examples.

Key Points for Persuasion:

- Use facts, quotes, outside research from experts, and illustrative examples to fully explain and support your main points.

- You must take an identifiable position on your topic and give reasons supported by persuasive information.

- Argument answers the opposition and predicts consequences.

Critical Writing

Critical writing involves analyzing and evaluating multiple sources to build an argument or to identify gaps in the research that has been widely accepted by professionals in a particular discipline. In the analysis phase, you examine and deconstruct ideas to find relationships that compare or contrast to your own thoughts about a topic or issue in your discipline.

In the evaluation phase, your task is to make conclusions about your analysis by judging sources according to a set of criteria or standards to identify strengths and weaknesses in the author's line of reasoning. In graduate school, the point of critical writing is to determine if the conclusions of an individual writer's work or an entire school of thought is justified based on the evidence they used to produce their research, theory or hypothesis.

Literature reviews and **annotated bibliographies** are **examples of critical writing assignments** that most graduate students encounter early on in their programs of study.

Academic Writer Survey

1. **I would describe my writing skills as...**
   - Strong. I consider myself a very good writer.
   - Okay. I am a decent writer, but there's room for improvement.
   - Marginal. Writing can be a difficult task for me.

2. **Have you used an assignment calculator?**
   - Yes. It's a very helpful tool for completing assignments.
   - I've heard of assignment calculators, but I've never used one.
   - I'm not familiar with assignment calculators, but it sounds interesting.

3. **Do you actively seek out ways to improve your writing?**
   - Yes. I believe there's always room for improvement.
   - Sometimes. I welcome feedback, but don't actively seek it.
   - No. I'm as good a writer as I'm ever going to be.

4. **Are you familiar with web-based tutoring?**
   - Yes. I've used web-based tutoring before.
   - I'm familiar with web-based tutoring, but have never used it.
   - I'm not familiar with web-based tutoring.

5. **What's your experience with online source matching tools?**
   - I have used online source matching tools throughout my academic career.
   - I know what they are, but have never used one.
   - I'm not familiar with source matching tools.

Assignment Calculator Example

Research Paper

Plan Your Assignment

Start Date *

| 09/17/2020 |

Due Date *

| 09/25/2020 |

Calculate

MM/DD/YYYY (e.g. 12/31/2020)

Sign in for due date notification options

By September 17, 2020: Understand assignment. Select topic.

Note: The research and writing process is not always linear. Keep in mind you may need to go forward or backwards.

- Read through and understand your assignment (from UNC).
  - Email or visit your instructor's office hours with questions.
- Select a workable topic (from Colorado State).
- Conduct preliminary investigation into topic using Google or other web searches. Work to understand your topic and the issues surrounding it.
  - Try a specialized online encyclopedia.
  - Get background on current topics using online tools like CQ Researcher or Opposing Viewpoints in Context.
  - Write down 5-10 keywords about your topic including terms, jargon, events, people, places, etc. to use as keywords or search terms when you do more searching for sources.

Percent time spent on this step: **8%**

Snapshot from the *University of Minnesota* assignment calculator

Chapter Three
Your Grammar Skills

Photo by Esther Muñoz Trilla from Pexels.

Good Grammar is Essential

In order to succeed in your program of study, you must enter with above average grammar and writing skills. At this level, faculty do not expect to teach fundamental writing or research skills, and most programs do not offer entry level writing classes. However, advanced written assignments comprise the majority of the assessments in graduate school, not objective tests or quizzes. Therefore, you must prepare yourself for the rigors of academic research by boosting your writing skills on a continual basis.

Just like with any skill, writing gets a bit easier with practice. Practice does not include cobbling together a paper at the last minute hoping to get a passing grade. If you wait until an assignment is due to write, your probabilities of successfully passing your class or getting approval for your thesis or dissertation dramatically decreases. Instead, successful writing practice includes working through grammar books, taking self-assessments and quizzes, or taking an online class with dynamic video lessons, whichever method best fits your learning style.

Luckily, there are several reputable resources to choose from when selecting the grammar and writing practice methods that suit you, some of which are highlighted at the end of this book. Before launching full steam into your graduate program, make sure that you have defined and reviewed each concept below as a first step in your writing skill improvement plan.

Parts of Speech

In order to write good sentences, you must know the building blocks of the written word in order to communicate complex ideas. Basically, parts of speech define the functions of the words that are used to create sentences. Review each of the parts below to understand how they combine to form thoughtful sentences, paragraphs and longer pieces of writing.

• Adjectives	• Nouns
• Adverbs	• Prepositions
• Articles	• Pronouns
• Conjunctions	• Verbs
• Interjections	

Punctuation

Punctuation are the marks used to separate elements within a sentence, to separate complete sentences, and to clarify the meaning within a sentence.

- Periods
- Question Marks
- Exclamation Points
- Commas
- Semicolons
- Colons
- Apostrophes
- Hyphens and Dashes
- Double and single quote marks
- Italics

Sentence Structure

A **sentence** is a group of words that includes a **subject** and a **verb (predicate)**. A sentence expresses a complete thought.

- In basic sentence structure, the subject comes first followed by the verb. Additional **complements**, (phrases or descriptions that complete or enhance the sentence), usually follow the verb.

Basic Sentence Structure:

- **Subject + Verb + Object/Complement/Phrase/Clause** (completion of the statement) = **(a complete sentence)**.

Sentence Types

Simple Sentence:

Like all complete sentences, a **simple sentence** contains a subject and a verb (predicate). A simple sentence is composed of only one independent clause. Therefore, a simple sentence contains one subject-predicate unit and no dependent clauses.

<u>Craig</u> <u>plays</u> the alto saxophone in a community jazz band.

- **Complete Subject** = <u>Craig</u>
- **Complete Predicate** = <u>plays</u> the alto saxophone in a community jazz band.

Compound Sentence:

A **compound sentence** consists of two complete sentences (two independent clauses) joined by a coordinating conjunction.

<u>Carl</u> <u>owns</u> a large collection of comic books, **but** <u>he</u> rarely <u>reads</u> them.

{Sentence 1}	{Sentence 2}
Carl owns a large collection of comic books.	He rarely reads them.

Complex Sentence:

A **complex sentence** contains one complete sentence (independent clause) and one or more dependent clauses. Even if the clauses are removed, one complete sentence still remains.

Complex Sentence:
When Tricia received the estimate for repairs, she decided to sell the car.

{Dependent Clause}	{Sentence 1}
When Tricia received the estimate for repairs,	she decided to sell the car.

Compound-Complex Sentence:

A **compound-complex sentence** contains two complete sentences (independent clauses) and at least one dependent clause. Deleting the dependent clauses does not affect the two complete sentences.

Before the game started, **Freddy cooked** buffalo wings and **Tanisha poured** drinks for everybody.

{Dependent Clause}	{Sentence 1}	{Sentence 2}
Before the game started,	Freddy cooked buffalo wings.	Tanisha poured drinks for everybody.

What areas of grammar do you need to work on?

Grammar Assessment

Directions: Answer each question to the best of your ability.

1.   Most_____in the Northeast have public transportation systems.
       a. citys
       b. cities
       c. city

2.   Steve had to buy Christmas gifts for several of his_____.
       a. brothers-in-law
       b. brother-in-law
       c. brother-in-laws

3.   Jonathan and_____thought that skydiving might be fun to try.
       a. I
       b. me
       c. her

4.   Everyone must bring_____own chair to the outdoor jazz concert.
       a. their
       b. our
       c. his or her

5.   The company launched_____new environmental campaign today.
       a. its
       b. their
       c. it's

6.   When LeBron dunked the ball into the net, the fans_____wild.
       a. go
       b. went

7.   By the time Chad is finished cramming for finals, he_____for seven
       hours.
       a. studied
       b. will have studied

8. As he dashed through the parking lot toward the building, Charles hoped that the meeting had not already_____.
   a. begun
   b. begin
   c. began

9. The coins in the jar on top of the microwave_____to be counted and rolled.
   a. needs
   b. need
   c. needed

10. One of those sandwiches in the refrigerator_____for you.
    a. is
    b. are
    c. not

11. Choose the sentence in which all the commas are used correctly.
    a. The 1985 Ford which has ignition trouble is hard to start.
    b. The 1985 Ford, which has ignition trouble is hard to start.
    c. The 1985 Ford, which has ignition trouble, is hard to start.

12. Choose the sentence in which all the commas are used correctly.
    a. Robert, my buddy from college, is now the registrar.
    b. Applicants, who arrive after four o'clock will have to return tomorrow.
    c. We synchronized our watches, and left.

13. Choose the sentence in which all the commas are used correctly.
    a. Your plan for a day-care center by the way, is the best I have ever seen.
    b. Your plan for a day-care center, by the way is the best I have ever seen.
    c. Your plan for a day-care center, by the way, is the best I have ever seen.

Directions: Cross out and correct all of the misspelled words.

14. The morning star seemed to loose some of it's brilliance.

15. Marci has trouble excepting complements; she blushes and becomes quite.

16. Is you're brother taking the teaching position he was offered?

Directions: Choose the correct synonym for #17-20.

17. Occupation is another word for_____.
   a. home
   b. job
   c. associate

18. Something that is benign is_____.
   a. cancerous
   b. dangerous
   c. non-threatening

19. There is a huge_____between the rich and the poor.
   a. chasm
   b. porch
   c. bridge

20. Please_____that noisy group.
   a. refer
   b. arrest
   c. expel

Directions: Correct all capitalization, grammar, punctuation, and spelling errors in the sentences below. Write "C" in the space provided if there are no errors.

21. Helen past the GED exem, and became a grate call center supervisor.

22. Duncan Haynes was late for work today, which was unusual.

23. Ms. greene are going to the supply closet to get some paper.

24. jerome is a vegetarian, but he love Chilli Cheese fries.

25. Although she pretends to like it Adrianne dont like going to company lunch's Potlucks or holiday parties.

Answers: Grammar Assessment

1. Most_____in the Northeast have public transportation systems.
   a. citys
   <u>b. cities</u>
   c. city

2. Steve had to buy Christmas gifts for several of his_____.
   <u>a. brothers-in-law</u>
   b. brother-in-law
   c. brother-in-laws

3. Jonathan and_____thought that skydiving might be fun to try.
   <u>a. I</u>
   b. me
   c. her

4. Everyone must bring_____own chair to the outdoor jazz concert.
   a. their
   b. our
   <u>c. his or her</u>

5. The company launched_____new environmental campaign today.
   <u>a. its</u>
   b. their
   c. it's

6. When LeBron dunked the ball into the net, the fans_____wild.
   a. go
   <u>b. went</u>

7. By the time Chad is finished cramming for finals, he_____for seven hours.
   a. studied
   <u>b. will have studied</u>

8. As he dashed through the parking lot toward the building, Charles hoped
   that the meeting had not already_____.
   a. begun
   b. begin
   c. began

9. The coins in the jar on top of the microwave_____to be counted and
   rolled.
   a. needs
   b. need
   c. needed

10. One of those sandwiches in the refrigerator_____for you.
    a. is
    b. are
    c. not

11. Choose the sentence in which all the commas are used correctly.
    a. The 1985 Ford which has ignition trouble is hard to start.
    b. The 1985 Ford, which has ignition trouble is hard to start.
    c. The 1985 Ford, which has ignition trouble, is hard to start.

12. Choose the sentence in which all the commas are used correctly.
    a. Robert, my buddy from college, is now the registrar.
    b. Applicants, who arrive after four o'clock will have to return
       tomorrow.
    c. We synchronized our watches, and left.

13. Choose the sentence in which all the commas are used correctly.
    a. Your plan for a day-care center by the way, is the best I have ever
       seen.
    b. Your plan for a day-care center, by the way is the best I have ever
       seen.
    c. Your plan for a day-care center, by the way, is the best I have ever
       seen.

Directions: Cross out and correct all of the misspelled words.

14. The morning star seemed to ~~loose~~ **(lose)** some of ~~it's~~ **(its)** brilliance.

15. Marci has trouble ~~excepting~~ **(accepting)** ~~complements~~; **(compliments)** she blushes and becomes ~~quite~~ **(quiet)**.

16. Is ~~you're~~ **(your)** brother taking the teaching position he was offered?

17. Occupation is another word for_____.
    a. home
    b. **job**
    c. associate

18. Something that is benign is_____.
    a. cancerous
    b. dangerous
    c. **non-threatening**

19. There is a huge_____between the rich and the poor.
    a. **chasm**
    b. porch
    c. bridge

20. Please_____that noisy group.
    a. refer
    b. arrest
    c. **expel**

Chapter Four
Your Research Skills

Photo by Fizkes from Can Stock Photo.

What is Research?

You might not realize it, but you are already a researcher. Every day, you search for answers to questions that require information you do not already possess. Perhaps you want to know about local farmer's markets or the best mechanic for brake jobs in your area. Comparison shopping for best quality or lowest prices is also a form of research. In graduate school, those same search and discover skills are used to perform academic research.

In educational settings, research equates to looking for information in outside sources, such as journal articles or scholarly books to enhance your essays or reports. Online research is now the most common and convenient way to conduct research, although public and school libraries still offer a variety of resources for academic research. Ultimately, the purpose for research is to increase your knowledge and understanding of a particular topic that you will communicate through papers, reports, and other written assignments.

Key Points to Remember:

- Research is about finding information from outside sources.
- Online research is common, but not the only way to search.
- Public and school libraries offer research resources.
- Only use trustworthy, reputable and authoritative sources.

Basic Steps of the Research Process

As you develop a routine for completing research assignments, you will undoubtedly create a method that works best for you. However, this brief overview outlines chronological steps and specific activities you will perform whenever you set about to conduct academic research.

Step 1: Identify and develop your topic.

If your instructor does not provide topic choices, choose an area that interests you.

Step 2: Do a preliminary search for information.

Once you decide on a topic, make sure enough information exists in book catalogs, periodical databases, and internet search engines to support your argument.

Step 3: Locate research materials.

Use electronic periodical databases to find magazine, newspaper, and journal articles. Choose the databases and source formats (e.g. print or digital) best suited to your particular topic through your institution's library or a local public library.

Step 4: Evaluate your sources.

Make sure that the sources you choose provide credible, truthful, and reliable information.

Step 5: Make notes.

From the sources you have chosen, note the information that will be useful in your paper. Be sure to document all the sources you consult, even if you do not use that particular source in your paper. The author, title, publisher, URL, page numbers and volume numbers will be needed later when creating a bibliography.

Step 6: Organize your information.

Begin by organizing the information you have collected. Gather your sources, your thoughts, and prepare to start writing. Consider the required page length and assignment criteria while you draft your paper to avoid any problems with your instructor.

Step 7: Write your paper.

This stage is the scariest and most frustrating for many writers, especially for those returning to graduate school after a long absence. Instead of trying to write the paper in chronological order—introduction, body, conclusion—discover the part that is easiest to begin with, but make sure to maintain logical order in your paragraphs and train of thought.

Step 8: Revise and edit your draft.

Now that you have written a draft that meets the assignment requirements, you must go back through your paper and correct all errors. Rearrange or delete sentences as needed, until your paper is properly organized and well supported with evidence from your outside sources. At this point, you also want to finalize your bibliography or references page.

Step 9: Cite your sources properly.

Give proper credit to the authors of the sources you include in your paper. Citing sources reduces the occurrence of plagiarism and allows readers to locate your sources. All of your sources should be listed in your bibliography according to an academic style guide such as APA or MLA.

Step 10: Proofread your work.

Always proofread. Do not skip this step! Print out a copy of your paper and correct all errors on the page. Make corrections on your digital copy as needed. Errors are easier to catch on paper than on screen, so do not solely rely on editing from a computer screen.

Checklist for Research Source Evaluation

When choosing sources for your research paper, use the CARS method of evaluation to evaluate their reliability.

Credibility	Check the author's credentials to determine if the information is trustworthy. Are they respected in their field of study?
Accuracy	The information in the source should be current, factual, detailed, exact, comprehensive, truthful, and objective.
Reasonableness	Engages the subject matter thoughtfully in a fair, balanced and truthful manner without personal bias.
Support	Provides convincing evidence to support its argument. References other reliable sources in a bibliography.

Important Research Terms

Direct Quotations provide a writer's exact words inside quotation marks.	**Example (Direct):** Albert Einstein said, "Logic will get you from A to B. Imagination will take you everywhere."
Indirect quotations give the meaning of an author's words without using quotation marks.	**Example (Indirect):** Albert Einstein said that imagination is boundless, and will take you everywhere.
A **summary** is a short paragraph that describes the main idea and supporting points of a longer work. It is written in your own words and does not include direct quotations.	**Plagiarism** is using someone else's words without giving them proper credit in your essay. Basically, plagiarism is stealing another writer's work.
APA Bibliography APA is a research documentation style created by the **American Psychological Association**. A **bibliography page** is the last page of an APA essay that lists all of the outside sources used within your paper.	**MLA/ Works Cited** MLA is a research documentation style created by the **Modern Language Association**. A **works cited page** is the last page of an MLA essay that lists all of the outside sources used within your paper.
Search engines are pages on the internet that use key words to locate other websites. Researchers use search engines to find information on the internet.	**Evaluation** of a web site involves studying it to make sure the information is accurate, up-to-date and fair.
Paraphrase means to reword information from an original source using your own words, without using direct quotations.	**Original Text:** Albert Einstein said, "Logic will get you from A to B. Imagination will take you everywhere."
	Paraphrase: Albert Einstein said that logic is limited, but imagination is boundless.

Research & Learning Skills Survey

1. Have you used an online academic library in the past?
   - Yes
   - No

2. Can you describe the types of resources that you are likely to find in an academic library?
   - Yes
   - No

3. Can you describe the kinds of resources available through subject-specific databases which are generally not available over the open internet?
   - Yes
   - No

4. Do you know how to define a topic for a graduate research paper?
   - Yes
   - No

5. Do you know how to adjust (narrow or broaden) the scope of your topic?
   - Yes
   - No

6. Do you know how to generate keywords to use in a topic search?
   - Yes
   - No

7. Do you know how to effectively use a single-box database search?
   - Yes
   - No

8. Do you know how to use the words **AND** and **OR** to effectively adjust the scope of a multi-box database search?
   - Yes
   - No

9. Can you describe criteria that can be used to assess the academic credibility of a source?
   - Yes
   - No

10. Can you describe how you would assess the bias of a source?
    - Yes
    - No

How well does each of the following statements represent your personal point of view?

11. I prefer to figure out the best way to do something.
    - Not at all
    - Somewhat
    - Absolutely

12. When I encounter a problem I cannot solve, I actively look for help.
    - Not at all
    - Somewhat
    - Absolutely

13. I know how to approach a subject that is unfamiliar to me.
    - Not at all
    - Somewhat
    - Absolutely

14. I usually base my reading approach on the purpose for my assignment.
    - Not at all
    - Somewhat
    - Absolutely

Chapter Five

The Writing Process

Photo by nappy from Pexels.

What is the Writing Process?

The steps of the writing process take you from a blank page to a written document. Instead of just staring at a computer screen and waiting for inspiration, sometimes you have to start small by jotting down words, phrases and finally, complete sentences. The six major steps of the writing process actually include several micro-activities that are meant to ease you into writing a full-length document. Although some resources cite more (or fewer) than six steps, the following are generally agreed upon in most reference books:

Steps of the Writing Process:

1. Exploring Ideas
2. Prewriting
3. Organizing
4. Writing
5. Revising
6. Producing the Final Copy

Step One: Exploring Ideas

Exploring ideas and prewriting blend into each other, and are often grouped into one stage instead of two separate ones. This is the first stage of the writing process where you can explore your initial ideas about a subject. The main goal of exploring ideas is to get your thoughts down on paper. To guide your brainstorming, provide as much information as you can about these three things:

1. the **subject**—What are you writing about?
2. the **purpose**—Why are you talking about this subject matter?
3. the **audience**—Who will read your writing?

Step Two: Prewriting

Prewriting consists of strategies that help you generate ideas and main points of support for your topic. Prewriting is also commonly referred to as brainstorming where you jot down or list ideas in simple words or short phrases. The goal is to stir your thinking about the subject and inspire you to get your ideas down on paper before attempting to compose a full document.

Types of Prewriting:

- **Freewriting:** is when you allow yourself a specified amount of time to write anything that comes to mind about your topic with no regard to organization, grammar, or editing. While freewriting, your pen never stops or leaves the page.

- **Questioning:** involves providing answers to *The Five Ws and One H*, also referred to as *The Six Ws*: *Who? What? When? Where? Why? How?* Before undertaking complex tasks or writing assignments, step back and answer these six questions before moving ahead. Understanding the fundamental direction of your essay or research paper allows your writing to flow a lot easier.

- **Journaling:** involves using a notebook to write raw, private thoughts about your subject. This technique usually applies to personal, narrative, persuasive or fiction writing.

- **Clustering:** involves drawing circles labeled with words or phrases that present your ideas, and connecting them with branches. The main idea of your subject matter is centered in the middle circle. Each related idea that branches from it will become the main points in the body of your writing project.

Step Three: Organizing

No matter how long or short, every writing assignment must include a beginning, middle and end—**an introduction, body and conclusion**. This is the fundamental organizing structure for any writing project. The only thing that changes within this structure is the subject, style, complexity and length of the content, whether you are writing a two-paragraph discussion post or a thesis.

In the organizing phase of the writing process, you start thinking about what information will come first, next, and last. What background information will you put in the introduction? What are the three main points of your paper? What kinds of content or information will you include to illustrate those points in the body of your paper? How will you conclude? All of these considerations comprise the process of organizing your document. Basically, you are selecting the details to include in the final version of your document.

Step Four: Writing the First Draft

After planning and organizing, now you must write! Take the notes from your outline and formulate ideas into full sentences and paragraphs. Your writing does not need to be perfect at this point. Use your outline to fill in the content of your document. For some people, writing long-hand is a good way to start, because it keeps them from getting distracted by computer keyboards or alerts popping up on a screen. However, some people prefer to type out their first draft. Choose the writing technique that works best for you.

Step Five: Revising the Draft

In this stage, you want your writing to be as clear and error-free as possible. At this point in the writing process, you are trying to finalize the draft by adding, deleting, editing, or rearranging your content. You are putting all of your details in order and editing for clarity. If you are collaborating on a document, now is the time to incorporate comments and suggestions from your team. The goal of revising the draft is to get the document as clean as possible before producing the final copy.

Step Six: Producing the Final Copy

Depending on the sophistication of your writing project, getting to this final stage could take hours, days, months or years. For example, a thesis proposal could take three months or a dissertation could take six months to a year to complete. In either case, the goal is to get the final document ready for print and distribution.

Every step in the writing process is necessary. Attempting to skip steps will cost you a lot of time, money and frustration. Although it might seem daunting, following the steps in order will allow you to write faster and more efficiently.

1. Print out a typed draft of your paper. This should be your third time printing and reading the document.

2. Edit your document. Carefully read and examine the document for errors.

3. Use a red pen to help you see errors on the printed draft.

4. Correct all errors including typos, misspelled words, grammar, punctuation, incomplete sentences, omitted words, and other mistakes.

5. After making all edits to your writing, print another copy of the paper. This should be your fourth printed copy.

6. Proofread your paper. Remember, proofreading is not the same as editing. To learn more about the differences, get your copy of the book, *Proofreading Power: Skills & Drills* from www.arhampton.com.

7. Get another person to check your writing for errors.

8. If a second reader finds more errors, fix them and print your document for a fifth review.

9. Give yourself enough time to take a break and read the document again with fresh eyes.

10. Print and read the paper again—for the final time—to correct all errors before submitting the final copy.

Writing Process Exercise

Directions: Circle the correct answer.

1. The step of the writing process during which writers think, jot down ideas, and plan the paper is known as_____.
    a. proofreading
    b. prewriting
    c. revising

2. Which of the following tasks comes *after* writing the first draft?
    a. deciding which ideas to include
    b. arranging ideas in a plan or outline
    c. proofreading for grammar and spelling errors

Directions: Read the paragraph and then answer the questions that follow by circling the letter of the correct response.

You should join the Army National Guard for several reasons. For one thing, joining is a cheap way to get in shape. Not only is physical training free, but you actually get paid to do it! Also, being an Army National Guard member is interesting and action-packed. You'll get hands-on training in one or more of hundreds of exciting specialties. You'll get opportunities to increase your knowledge of fields like mechanics, law enforcement, computers, and communications. Along the way, you'll meet new people who share your desire for adventure, and you'll form friendships that will last a lifetime. If you join the Army National Guard, you will also learn leadership skills that you can use in your own community and in times of crisis, when you'll be called to action to perform rescue missions and help victims of disasters. By helping your fellow Americans, you'll be serving your country. In fact, that's the most important reason of all. Join the Army National Guard because we can't defend this country without you.

3. This paragraph was written for an audience of_____.
    a. senior citizens
    b. Army National Guard soldiers
    c. young men and women

4. The subject of this paragraph is_____.
    a. getting in shape
    b. joining the Army National Guard
    c. ways to satisfy a craving for adventure

5. The purpose of this paragraph is to_____.
    a. tell about the mission of the Army National Guard
    b. persuade people to join the Army National Guard
    c. convince Army National Guard soldiers that they made the right decision when they joined

Answers: Writing Process Exercise

1. **prewriting**

2. **proofreading for grammar and spelling errors**

3. **young men and women**

4. **joining the Army National Guard**

5. **persuade people to join the Army National Guard**

Chapter Six

Graduate Writing Standards

Photo by Clemence Taillez on Unsplash.

What is Graduate Level Writing?

When you write at the graduate level, you contribute to the conversation about a specific issue by adding to the body of knowledge on your topic. To contribute, you must first learn what has already been said about a given topic in the form of a literature review. As you review the literature, take note of important figures, theories, and controversies. Most importantly, note what is still unknown or what has not been said about your topic. With your work, focus on filling a gap in the literature and offering a new perspective. While classroom assignments may serve as the impetus for following a particular line of research, the ideas and arguments you write about should strive for wider relevance to your thesis or dissertation. As a graduate-level writer, you engage other scholars as peers, building on and challenging their ideas in order to advance the knowledge base in your program of study. Far from being a simple assessment of ability, graduate-level writing extends beyond the classroom and seeks to impact the broader academic community.

Unless otherwise noted, most written assignments should follow these general guidelines:

Style & Tone Quicklist

- Times New Roman, 12-point font
- Double-spaced.
- One-inch margins all around.
- Page numbers (See style guide).
- Abstract: 350 words maximum
- Formal third person academic writing style.
- Do not use first or second person, such as "I," "you," "we," or "us."
- Check with your instructor or department for specifics.

Third Person

In academic writing, you will most often use third person. Writing in third person means using formal language and more sophisticated vocabulary to express a particular perspective or point of view on a topic of interest. The third person academic writing style uses objective language and third person pronouns. For example, scholarly articles found in peer reviewed journals are common types of academic writing at the college/university level.

Third Person Pronouns:

- *he, him, his, himself*
- *she, her, hers, herself,*
- *it, its, itself,*
- *they, them, their, theirs, themselves*

Below are examples using third person language:

- Chapter four of Cooley's autobiography states that he was born out of wedlock.
- In the fourteenth century, English peasant farmers had to struggle to survive.
- Unfortunately, since there are so many possible explanations, the correct one is difficult to ascertain.
- These exercises can easily be incorporated into a daily routine, with each one being repeated several times.

Common Types of Writing Assignments

Discussion Post
- **Length:** A few paragraphs
- **Supporting sources:** 1-5 sources; may include peer-reviewed, professional, or non-scholarly sources.
- **Note:** Check the requirements closely. A reflective assignment may require no sources at all.

Long Paper Assignment
- **Length:** 6-20 or more pages
- **Supporting sources:** 10+ sources; may include peer-reviewed articles, book chapters, or books.

Dissertation
- **Length:** 100+ pages
- **Supporting Sources:** 50+ sources
- **Scholarly literature review:** predominantly peer-reviewed articles and books
- Reports, statistics, or case studies to supplement scholarly sources
- New, original data gathered from your own research

Short Paper Assignment
- **Length:** 5 pages or fewer
- **Supporting sources:** 3-10 sources; may include peer-reviewed, professional articles, book chapters, or periodicals.

Comprehensive Examination
- **Length:** 15+ pages per question.
- **Supporting sources:** 10+ sources per question; may include peer-reviewed articles, book chapters or periodicals.

Graduate Writing Guidelines

1. Report research in the past tense.

This error occurs frequently when students are completing an article review. When you refer to the work of others, use past tense (since the author has already written the article and already had it published).

2. Write in active voice.

Most academic writing is in the active voice. Sentences constructed in the active voice add impact to formal writing. With an active voice, the subject performs an action. Active sentences follow a clear subject + verb + object construct for reading ease.

Below are examples of sentences using active voice:

- The researchers gathered data on the effectiveness of distance education.
- Patients experienced shorter wait times when nurses worked more hours.
- Graduate students usually complete their programs in two years.

3. Avoid personification in academic writing.

The APA manual refers to this concept as *anthropomorphism,* but in grammar school, you might have learned it as *personification.* Anthropomorphism or personification, refers to writing that implies that inanimate objects have human characteristics or abilities. This mistake is often the result of writers trying to avoid the first person.

Wrong:

The **study** concluded... [a study cannot **DO** anything, since it is not human]

Right:

The **researcher** concluded... [a **person** must do the studying and concluding]

4. Use formal language.

Avoid any instances of colloquialisms. Less obvious than slang, some word choices are still too casual or informal for academic writing. Similarly, do not use text shorthand or emoticons in your work. While most people recognize that such shortcuts are not appropriate in research papers, some students do not realize that such informality is also inappropriate for discussion posts or courseroom email communications. Other expressions to avoid include "in conclusion", "in summary", or "the following."

5. Avoid writing about opinions or personal experiences.

Academic writing focuses on literature and research produced by a particular field of study. Therefore, your personal experiences or opinions should not be included in your argument. Since political or religious issues lean toward subjective bias, avoid these topics as a general rule, unless you are engaging in scholarship from these disciplines. So, do not use the phrase, "I feel," or any other first-person expressions in writings that do not require self-reflection.

6. Avoid biased language.

At the time of this writing, diversity and inclusion are under attack in the United States. However, there are still writers and editors in academia and all forms of media who want to genuinely and respectfully share the messages of humans from diverse cultures, racial backgrounds and orientations. The bottom line is to treat all people with dignity and respect. Do not refer to race, ethnicity, age, disability or sexual orientation unless **ABSOLUTELY** necessary, and when in doubt, ask—do not assume.

7. Check for consistency in verb tense.

Subject-verb agreement is one of the most prevalent mistakes in student writing. To avoid this error, become aware of the types of verbs in your sentences. Are they active or passive? Check for verb tense consistency across paragraphs and throughout the entire paper. Are you discussing events or research that occurred in the past or the present? Because action and states of activity are expressed through a wide variety of grammatical constructions, it is easy to commit subject-verb agreement errors, especially in long and complex sentences. So, remember to habitually make these corrections in the revising and editing phase of your writing process.

8. Use appropriate punctuation for formal writing.

Be aware that the formal tone of academic writing extends to punctuation as well. Do not use contractions in formal writing, unless they appear in direct quotations. Do not use emoticons or any punctuation commonly used in text messages or casual social media posts. Avoid using dashes or ellipses to set off parenthetical ideas when another type of punctuation, (such as a comma or parenthesis), is more appropriate for formal academic writing.

10. Use correct style guide formatting when citing sources.

While APA, MLA or CMOS references can be daunting for even experienced academic writers, it is important to familiarize yourself with the requirements for whichever one your instructor or institution chooses. The most common issues regarding reference citations occur in the body of the paper (especially parenthetical citations), and on the reference or bibliography page. Some disciplines have very specific recommendations of usage. For example, some fields allow first-person language while others highly discourage it. As such, it is your responsibility to familiarize yourself with academic style guidelines to resolve any formatting related questions.

Knowledge Check

1. At this point, I still need information on…

2. Regarding academic writing, I feel confident that I can…

Formal Writing Exercise

Directions: Reduce the informal writing style of the following sentences by replacing the **bold** phrase with one verb. (If you must, use a dictionary or thesaurus, but commit to building your vocabulary!)

Example:

Informal: Researchers *looked at* the way strain *builds up* around a fault.

Formal One-word Revision: Researchers *observed* the way strain *accumulates* around a fault.

---

1. Drug prescriptions for depression have **gone up** dramatically in the past decade.

2. Snack machines in school hallways **cut down** on wasted food in the cafeteria.

3. Researchers have **found out** that branding is a powerful tool which has a significant impact on both consumer buying patterns and company profits.

4. Overseas outsourcing will not completely **get rid** of the problem of costly tax burdens for U. S. corporations.

5. Accountants have long been **looking into** ways of reducing corporate taxation.

6. The issue of inadequate student lunches was **brought up** in the last *Parent Teacher Association* meeting.

7. Students demanded that college administrators **come up with** new ideas on improving employment opportunities for graduating seniors.

8. Enrollment at for-profit universities has been **going up and down** for the past two years.

9. Special occasion committees are **set up** to improve employee morale.

10. Stan **got his point across** with angry outbursts instead of compassion.

Answers: Formal Writing Exercise

1. Drug prescriptions for depression have ***gone up*** dramatically in the past decade.
   - Drug prescriptions for depression have *increased* dramatically in the past decade.

2. Snack machines in school hallways ***cut down*** on wasted food in the cafeteria.
   - Snack machines in school hallways *reduce* wasted food in the cafeteria.

3. Researchers have ***found out*** that branding is a powerful tool which has a significant impact on consumer buying patterns and company profits.
   - Researchers have *discovered* that branding is a powerful tool which has a significant impact on consumer buying patterns and company profits.

4. Overseas outsourcing will not completely ***get rid*** of the problem of costly tax burdens for U. S. corporations.
   - Overseas outsourcing will not completely *eliminate* the problem of costly tax burdens for U. S. corporations.

5. Accountants have long been ***looking into*** ways of reducing corporate taxation.
   - Accountants have long been *investigating* ways of reducing corporate taxation.

6. The issue of inadequate student lunches was ***brought up*** in the last *Parent Teacher Association* meeting.
   - The issue of inadequate student lunches was *discussed* in the last *Parent Teacher Association* meeting.

7. Students demanded that college administrators ***come up with*** new ideas on improving employment opportunities for graduating seniors.
   - Students demanded that college administrators *present (offer/propose)* new ideas on improving employment opportunities for graduating seniors.

8. Enrollment at for-profit universities has been ***going up and down*** for the past two years.
   - Enrollment at for-profit universities has been *fluctuating* for the past two years.

9. Special occasion committees are ***set up*** to improve employee morale.
   - Special occasion committees are *established (created)* to improve employee morale.

10. Stan ***got his point across*** with angry outbursts instead of compassion.
    - Stan *communicated* with angry outbursts instead of compassion.

Chapter Seven
Graduate Writing Style

Photo by Christina Morillo from Pexels.

Essential Graduate Writing Style Guidelines

At this point, you might be realizing that the demands for graduate level writing are pretty high, and you are correct. Graduate students often become dismayed early in their programs when confronted with so many advanced writing assignments, especially if their prior experiences did not properly prepare them for the challenges of professional writing. Instead of just reporting on a topic and sticking a few references throughout the paper, faculty at the graduate level expect for students to produce in-depth critical analyses of issues within their field of study. As mentioned earlier, this requires a shift in thinking from simply being a consumer of material written by others to becoming a producer of research that contributes to a larger conversation within a particular academic discipline. However, on a practical level, you need to know how to write graduate papers and what mistakes to avoid. To this end, the following guidelines offer tips and techniques to help you level up your academic writing skills.

Choose an Appropriate Level of Diction

Diction refers to word choice and the overall tone of your writing. Since scholarly writing is formal, you must avoid using slang or casual words and phrases. Informal writing can suggest to scholarly readers that you are not serious about the topic. Therefore, it is a good idea to regularly increase your vocabulary, because you cannot just breezily write the way you speak in academic environments.

On the other hand, do not simply use "big words" in order to seem intelligent. Beginning writers often haphazardly turn to a thesaurus to stock their writing with "smarter" sounding words. However, many words in a thesaurus have special, nuanced meanings that might not be an exact synonym for the word you are trying to replace. Considering this, diction also involves using the right words to fit the context of the ideas you are trying to express, so that your writing remains clear and concise.

Casual Writing:
- Participants showed up for four sessions, watched a film, and answered some questions.

Formal Writing:
- Participants attended four one-hour sessions, during which they viewed a 30-minute sexual harassment video and completed a brief survey.

Point of View

Certain **first-person** constructions, such as "I think" and "I believe," not only sound uncertain, but are also inherently redundant. If you are the author, the majority of your writing reflects something that you think or believe. While there might be rare occasions to identify a statement as a personal belief, your writing will be more direct and powerful if you avoid these reflexive qualifiers. Note in the example below how deleting the phrase "I think that" gives the statement a more authoritative tone.

Qualified Reflexive Statement:
- **I think that** workplace microaggressions are symptomatic of larger systemic issues of racial bias.

Unqualified Statement:
- Workplace microaggressions are symptomatic of larger systemic issues of racial bias.

Exceptions to First-Person

Although academic writing does not typically include first-person, it can be used when discussing research procedures. In fact, the new APA seventh edition guidelines insist that writers use the first-person pronoun "I" when describing research methods instead of "this author" or some other awkward reference to yourself. Likewise, if you conduct research activities with other people, you will refer to "we" in your writing.

Example:

- *I* designed an interactive social experiment that included 40 participants randomly chosen according to computer lab usage.

- At the end of the experiment, *we* filtered the results according to demographics and amount of usage.

Exceptions to Personal Experience

Since personal experience is generally discouraged in academic writing, you must get permission from your instructor or committee before using this kind of narrative. Permission might be granted if your experience is relevant to your thesis or dissertation.

However, if you choose to incorporate life experience as a form of support for your argument, make sure that your commentary is scholarly, formal and appropriate.

Example:

Incorrect First-Person:

- One time I was downtown and saw a bunch of guys gang up on this one black guy.

Correct First-Person:

- Having witnessed violence against African American males firsthand, I can attest to the implications of excessive force against their community.

Avoid Second Person

Do not use the second person construction "you" in academic writing. No exceptions. Instead, use **third person**.

Example:

- **(Second Person):** If you are experiencing joblessness, you often have no income other than weekly unemployment checks.

- **(Third Person):** Employees experiencing joblessness often have no income other than weekly unemployment checks.

Figures of Speech

Graduate-level writing tends to avoid figurative language like similes and metaphors. Other literary devices such as rhymes, puns, and heavy alliteration are also typically avoided.

Clichés are phrases that were once considered sharp and interesting, but have become dull and boring through overuse. Avoid clichés in your graduate-level writing since they detract from the formal tone of your writing.

Example of Clichés:

- **Beyond the shadow of a doubt,** some people can adjust to the **hustle and bustle** of city life more than others.

Correction:

- ~~Beyond the shadow of a doubt,~~ Some people can adjust to the ~~hustle and bustle~~ **energy and motion** of city life more than others.

- Some people can adjust to the **energy and motion** of city life more than others.

Rhetorical questions are used sparingly in academic writing. While they serve as effective signal phrases in casual writing or in oral presentations, rhetorical questions can appear patronizing to scholarly audiences. Instead of asking a question, you can usually frame the information as a statement.

Example of a Rhetorical Question:

- What do these results say about the population?

- **(As a Statement):** These results indicate several things about the population.

Avoid Bias

Generally, scholarly writing is objective and void of personal opinion to gain the respect and trust of the audience. One best practice is to select an exciting and challenging topic or current issue that encourages a problem-solving approach in order to maintain objectivity and to eliminate bias.

For example, the causes of racial discrimination in elementary education is a broad, triggering topic that provokes a range of strong emotional responses. However, using cultural and sensitivity training to reduce racial bias among elementary school teachers introduces a solution to a problem that can be analyzed and discussed more objectively.

Advanced Writing Guidelines

1. Clearly state the goal of your paper at the beginning. What is your paper about? What is the point? This is the information that readers look for in your introduction, not near the end or in the final conclusion. To avoid confusing the reader, provide full background information about your topic in the opening pages. If applicable, state whether the paper contains experiments, a literature review, a formal model, a new statistical method, charts, graphs or some combination of the above.

2. Write a concise thesis statement. Regardless of the length of your introduction, a clear thesis statement should appear at the end as a lead into your first body paragraph. Depending on the nature and complexity of the topic, some thesis statements might include all of the main points that will be covered in your paper, while others might imply the purpose and direction of your research.

3. Use concrete examples. In general, abstract theoretical concepts need to be clarified with descriptive, concrete examples. Transitional phrases such as "for instance" and "for example" signal to readers that an easy-to-understand illustration will follow. Specific examples work well in every section of a research paper including the introduction, the method section, and the discussion section.

4. Eliminate wordiness. Clear writing is easy to understand. Concise writing is direct and free of excess wording. Therefore, the goal of clear and concise academic writing is to incorporate narration, style, rhythm, and sentence variety to communicate as effectively as possible without overwhelming the reader. Techniques to achieve this level of conciseness include fixing choppy sentences, combining sentences and avoiding vague language—all of which are discussed in the book *Creative Business Writing* by Ashan R. Hampton.

5. When describing experiments, integrate your results along with their interpretations. Graduate students often summarize their findings in the results section and separately discuss the interpretation of their findings in the discussion section. Although this method may appear to be objective and scientific, it is not helpful. Having to flip to another section to fully understand your research will frustrate your audience. Instead, try to integrate the results and their interpretations as much as possible, providing maximum guidance for the reader. Minus the aforementioned interpretations, use the discussion section to summarize your findings, elaborate on alternative explanations, and connect your findings to other experiments, if applicable.

6. Increase structure and organization with subheadings. Graduate students often hesitate to add subheadings to their papers. However, effectively written subheadings break up long text and direct the reader to pertinent information, which improves the overall readability of your document.

7. Improve the flow of ideas with transitional phrases. Transitions are words or phrases that connect sentences to other sentences within paragraphs. They also connect paragraphs to other paragraphs. Overall, transitions help readers to follow your writing in logical order when you switch from one idea to another idea. Transitional phrases such as "However", "In contrast to", "To this end," or "In sum," connect what has been presented earlier to what will be presented next. In this way, ideas between sentences and paragraphs logically flow to the next. Phrases that indicate time, process, and results are particularly helpful.

8. Write concise sentences that focus on one idea. Sentences can get too long when they are wordy or stuffed with too many ideas. To avoid this, break ideas into manageable sentences of 17-21 words. Anything longer than that is too long. Also, keep paragraph lengths to approximately 10-12 sentences. The goal is to streamline your academic writing without sounding dull or robotic by effectively arranging words within your sentences and paragraphs.

9. Arrange information in paragraphs chronologically or from general to specific. In a well-organized paper, each sentence provides information that the next sentence elaborates on, so that the reader is never confused by unexpected changes in topic or emphasis. In order to achieve flow, the main rule is to start sentences with old information, and end with new information. This formula also applies to paragraphs.

Example:

- According to Smith (2011) *in HBCUs Must Embrace Online Education,* HBCUs are lagging behind trends toward distance education, which compromises their ability to effectively educate students. Although many HBCU administrators perceive online learning as integral to their long-term goals, as of spring 2020, only 18 percent of these 105 active institutions offer online courses.

10. Maintain focus in your conclusion. Summarize the main ideas of your paper in the conclusion. Do not introduce new information or ideas that have not already been mentioned. Depending on your topic, the conclusion is used to address any opposition to your argument or research methods. Basically, the conclusion is supposed to effectively round off your paper, not incite new discussions.

Chapter Eight
Writing Complex Paragraphs

Photo by NordWood Themes on Unsplash

What are Complex Paragraphs?

A paragraph is a group of related sentences that develop one main idea. All of the paragraphs in a written document must be on topic and properly organized in order for the writing to make sense to the reader. In graduate school writing, complex paragraphs should demonstrate a certain degree of critical thinking, research, and academic sophistication.

Complex paragraphs include five (5) main parts:

1. **Topic** Sentence
2. **Support:** Lead-in
3. **Support:** Quoted Research (Signal Phrase)
4. **Support:** Analysis (Summary/Paraphrase)
5. **Transition:** Concluding Sentence

As with any other paragraph, a complex paragraph must begin with a topic sentence to establish the main idea of the paragraph. All of the sentences after the topic sentence count as support.

Analysis: Additional information that enlightens the reader or gives them other points to consider that can lead to an enhanced understanding of how the idea in the quote relates to the main idea of your paper. Analysis consists of your own interpretations and observations about the topic without using the personal pronoun "I", or phrases like *"I think"* or *"I feel"*. Instead of leaving a quote from outside sources hanging, always support them with a sentence or two of analysis, summary or paraphrase.

Transitional Phrases:

- The last line of the paragraph should bridge into the next related idea that will be discussed in the next paragraph.

- Use transitional words and phrases, such as "in addition to," "next," "unlike previous findings," or other similar phrases.

Breakdown: Complex Paragraphs

TOPIC SENTENCE: The student population within higher education is rapidly changing. **LEAD-IN:** Gone are the days of the ruddy faced freshmen leaving their homes to experience their first taste of independence without parental intervention or control. In contrast, today's college students are more experienced, slightly older, socioeconomically disadvantaged and academically challenged. **QUOTED RESEARCH:** In a *Chronicle of Higher Education* article, "Raising Graduation Rates Involves More Than Just Colleges," Espinosa (2010) describes these 21st century learners as, "those from growing racial and ethnic minority groups, those who are the first in their families to attend college, adult learners, and displaced workers." **ANALYSIS:** Unfortunately, these millennial students are also products of a broken, chaotic public education system that has rendered them unprepared for college level curriculums. However, the current economic crisis demands that workers possess higher skill levels and college degrees in order to become successful in today's fast-paced, global workplaces. **TRANSITION:** As a result, more workers feel the pressure to enter college, and colleges feel the pressure to accommodate students who are academically unready for college life.

My Notes:_____

Types of Support

Support for complex paragraphs can include:

- Anecdotes (Personal Examples)
- Quotes
- Statistics
- Authoritative Sources
- Scientific Research

Anecdotes/Personal Examples

- **Anecdotes:** Brief stories from personal experience, history or popular culture found in literature, magazines, books or other printed media. Using extended examples can pique interest in your topic, as well as add additional support to your essay.

Example:

Many institutions are struggling to make payroll amid reduced state and federal funding. For example, the President of Southern Illinois University encouraged campus officials to curtail non-salary spending to protect the university's ability to meet its payroll (Southern Illinois U. Cuts Spending, 2009).

Quotes

- **Quotes:** Sentences taken from another author's writing exactly as written, word for word or verbatim. Journals, magazines, research reports and newspapers are common reference sources for pulling quotes to use in the body of an essay. A **signal phrase** is created whenever you mention an author's name, organization or publication before citing, summarizing or paraphrasing the actual quote. If you do not mention the author or title of the source, you must include that information in a proper in-text citation.

Example:

On the other hand, Stuart (2010) contends that many HBCUs are incapable of closing the digital divide. Stuart flatly states, "Closing the so-called digital divide is becoming less of a possibility for many HBCUs." He cites lack of finances as a primary reason for HBCUs lack of adequate technological infrastructure to support online learning or campus wide Wi-Fi.

Statistics

- **Statistics:** Bits of information that use numbers to highlight various research studies and reports.

Example:

According to Smith (2011) in *HBCUs Must Embrace Online Education,* HBCUs are lagging behind the distance education trend. Although many HBCU administrators perceive online learning as integral to their long-term goals, only 18 percent of these 105 active institutions offer online courses. In comparison, 66 percent of the nation's postsecondary institutions offer college-level distance education courses, according to the U.S. Department of Education.

Authoritative Sources

- **Authoritative Sources:** Scholarly articles, books, or other academic publications written by researchers or notable leaders in their field of study.

Example:

In her book, *Black Feminist Thought: Knowledge, Consciousness, and the Politics of Empowerment* (1990), Patricia Hill Collins writes, "Depending on historical time and place, African American women employed a range of strategies in challenging the rules governing our subordination. In many cases, Black women practiced individual protest against unfair rules and practices (p.155).

Scientific Research

- **Scientific Research:** Objective reports or articles that inform the public of facts or innovations in a particular field of study that often include numerical data or statistics.

Example:

In the article, "Covid-19 and Cancer" (2020), Norman E. Sharpless, the director of the U.S. National Cancer Institute, gives an ominous warning about the future of cancer research. Sharpless states, "Beyond clinical care, the COVID-19 pandemic has caused an unprecedented disruption throughout the cancer research community, shuttering many labs and slowing down cancer clinical trial operations. Many scientists and clinicians are pivoting their cancer research activities to study the impact of SARS-CoV-2 on cancer. The scientific community must ensure that this pause is only temporary, because trials are the only way to make progress in developing new therapies for cancer. Given the long time-line between basic cancer research and changes to cancer care, the effects of pausing research today may lead to slowdowns in cancer progress for many years to come" (p. 1290).

Summary or Paraphrase

- **Summary:** A type of support that includes giving a general overview of the main points of a longer piece of writing in your own words.

- **Paraphrase:** A type of support that involves restating the main ideas of outside sources in your own words, without distorting the original meaning of the author's writing.

Summaries and paraphrases are often linked together and follow the same principles of not plagiarizing or copying someone else's work, word for word. More in-depth explanations and examples of summarizing and paraphrasing will follow in the next chapter.

Key Points:

- Include quotes from outside research sources.
- Cite sources correctly with in-text citations.
- Offer analysis, summary or paraphrase to fully explain your points.
- Write effective transition statements.
- Only Include the sources you actually cite within your paper in the bibliography or reference page.

Complex Paragraph Exercise

Directions: Read the paragraph and answer the questions that follow.

(1) Playing video games may give doctors an advantage in the operating room, helping them save lives. (2) A 2004 study at New York's Beth Israel Medical Center tested thirty-three doctors on video game tasks that measured their motor skills, reaction time, and hand-eye coordination. (3) These are the same skills that are essential to performing laparoscopic surgery, which involves using a joystick to maneuver a tiny video camera inserted into a patient's body. (4) Researchers found that doctors who played video games for more than three hours a week were 37 percent less likely than non-gamers to make mistakes. (5) The gamer doctors also finished procedures 27 percent faster than non-gamers.

1. Give the number of the topic sentence in the paragraph above. _____

2. Which sentence(s) include statistics? _____

3. Which sentence includes a signal phrase? _____

4. Which sentence counts as analysis? _____

Chapter Nine
Summarizing, Paraphrasing & Quoting

Photo by Andrea Piacquadio from Pexels.

What is a Summary?

- A **summary** is an overview of the major ideas of an article or longer publication that is shorter than the original text. Basically, you are describing the main ideas of an entire source in your own words.

- Before you can summarize a text, you must re-read it until you fully understand it.

- Highlight the first sentence in each paragraph to map out the author's main points. Remember, a topic sentence is the first sentence in a paragraph that should introduce the main idea of a paragraph.

- Focus on the author's main ideas, not minor supporting details when developing your summary.

Example: Summary

Original passage:

Language is the main means of communication between peoples. But, with so many different foreign tongues, language has become a barrier rather than an aid to understanding among cultures. For many years, people have dreamed of setting up an international, universal language which all people could speak and understand. The arguments in favor of a universal language are simple and obvious. If all peoples spoke the same tongue, cultural and economic ties might be much closer, and good will might increase between around the world (Kispert, 1990). However, opponents argue that cultural uniqueness will be compromised if everyone is forced to speak one language.

Summary:

People communicate mainly through language; however, having so many different languages creates communication barriers. Some think that one universal language could bring countries together culturally and economically and also increase good feelings among them (Kispert, 1990). However, opponents argue that speaking one language will diminish cultural identity.

What is Paraphrasing?

- A **paraphrase** of a text only uses words, phrases or sentences from the original source. When paraphrasing, you are incorporating information from an outside source into your own writing.

- A paraphrase is NOT a direct quote, and therefore does not include quotation marks.

- The goal is to weave paraphrased material into your own sentences and paragraphs.

Example: Paraphrase

Original passage:

Language is the main means of communication between peoples. But, with so many different foreign tongues, language has become a barrier rather than an aid to understanding among cultures. For many years, people have dreamed of setting up an international, universal language which all people could speak and understand. The arguments in favor of a universal language are simple and obvious. If all peoples spoke the same tongue, cultural and economic ties might be much closer, and good will might increase between around the world (Kispert, 1990). However, opponents argue that cultural uniqueness will be compromised if everyone is forced to speak one language.

Paraphrase:

Humans communicate through language. However, because there are so many languages in the world, language is an obstacle rather than an aid to communication. For a long time, people have wished for an international language that speakers all over the world could understand, because a universal language would build cultural and economic bonds. It would also create better feelings among countries (Kispert, 1990). However, opponents argue that cultural uniqueness will dissolve into conformity.

What is a Quote?

- A **quote** is a word, phrase, sentence or paragraph that has been directly copied, verbatim, into your own writing.

- **Direct quotes** that are written just as the author stated word-for-word are surrounded by quotation marks.

- Quotes are paired with **in-text citations**, which might include the author's last name, page number or year of publication. The way you format quotes and in-text citations depends on your style guide (e.g. APA or MLA).

Example: Direct Quotes

(Words): Using Gladwell's terms, some important differences exist between *"explicit"* learning and *"collateral"* learning (36).

(Phrases): Tomorrow's educators need to understand the distinction between, as Gladwell puts it, "two very different kinds of learning" (36).

(Sentences): As Gladwell argues, "Meta-analysis of hundreds of studies done on the effects of homework shows that the evidence supporting the practice is, at best, modest" (36).

What is a Long or Block Quote?

- A **quote** that is longer than three lines is considered a **long quote.**

- **Long quotes** should be formatted as **block quotes.**

- A **block quote** is indented 10 spaces (two keyboard tabs) from the left margin.

- A **block quote** must be followed by sentences that explain it and connect it to the ideas of your topic. Otherwise, it becomes a hanging quote.

- Do not leave **block quotes** hanging without additional statements of analysis and support.

Example: Block Quotes

A child is unlikely to acquire collateral learning through books or studying for the SAT exams, Gladwell explains. They do acquire it through play, even playing video games:

> The point is that books and video games represent two very different kinds of learning. When you read a biology textbook, the content of what you read is what matters. Reading is a form of explicit learning. When you play a video game, the value is in how it makes you think. Video games are an example of collateral learning, which is no less important. ("Brain" 2)

In asserting that collateral learning "is no less important" than explicit learning, Gladwell implies that American education may be producing students who are imbalanced—with too much content knowledge and too little facility in dealing with unstructured situations, the kinds of situations that a person is likely to face every day of his or her working life.

Incorporating Sources into Your Paragraphs

- From previous examples of **summarizing, paraphrasing and quoting**, you might recognize a pattern in how they are inserted into a paragraph.

- The **four components below** are necessary to properly incorporate sources into your own work:

Signal Phrase → Quote, Paraphrase or Summary → In-text Citation → Connection to Main Ideas

Incorporating Sources Example:

As Malcolm Gladwell reminds us, many American schools have eliminated recess in favor of more math and language studies, favoring "explicit" learning over "collateral" learning ("Brain" 36). This approach is problematic, because it takes away children's opportunities to interact socially and problem-solve, which are critical skills in today's world.

Four Source Components Highlighted:

(Signal Phrase) As Malcolm Gladwell reminds us, many American schools have eliminated recess in favor of more math and language studies, favoring (Source Material): "explicit" learning over "collateral" learning (In-text Citation) ("Brain" 36). (Connection/Analysis): This approach is problematic, because it takes away children's opportunities to interact socially and problem-solve, which are critical skills in today's world.

Connecting Ideas

When connecting source material with your own ideas at the end of a quote, your connection (meaning your analysis or commentary) can do one of the following:

1. Emphasize a key point from the quoted material.
2. Expand on the source material's main idea.
3. Connect the source material to your ideas on the topic.
4. Rephrase the main point of the source in simpler terms.

Key Points

- A **summary** gives an overview of an entire source.
- A **summary** is shorter than the original text.
- A **paraphrase** only uses a small portion of a source.
- A **paraphrase** focuses on short passages from source material.

Summarizing, Paraphrasing & Quoting Exercise

Directions: Circle the letter of the correct answer for each of the following questions.

1. The main idea and supporting points of a longer work, presented in the writer's own words, is called_____
    a. a direct quotation.
    b. a summary.
    c. plagiarism.

2. Another word for *plagiarism* is_____
    a. summarizing.
    b. quoting.
    c. stealing.

3. Which of the following does *not* involve paraphrasing?
    a. writing a summary
    b. giving a direct quotation
    c. giving an indirect quotation

4. Which of the following belongs in a summary?
    a. the summary writer's personal opinions
    b. the author, title, and source of the original
    c. related ideas that were not in the original source

5. Which of the following should appear in *both* a direct quotation and an indirect quotation?
    a. the name of the writer and a reference to the source
    b. quotation marks
    c. the word *that*

Directions: Below are two sources followed by passages from student papers. If the student has summarized, directly quoted, or paraphrased the source correctly, write "**C**" for **correct** on the blank. If the source is incorrectly used or cited, write "I" for **"incorrect."**

"A generation ago, it was considered rude to eat in front of others in public. Now, Americans eat everywhere, all day long—an average of five meals a day, counting snacks. Cars have cupholders, but they arguably need trays, too. Americans eat 30 meals a year in their vehicles."

—Brink, S. (2005, March). Eat this now! *U.S. News & World Report*, 57.

_____ 6. **Student version:** Americans no longer confine themselves to eating at home. As a matter of fact, Susan Brink says that a generation ago, it was considered rude to eat in front of others. Now, though, Americans eat thirty meals a year in their vehicles.

_____ 7. **Student version:** According to Susan Brink in the article, "Eat This Now!" (2005), eating in front of others was once believed to be rude, but now Americans are in the habit of eating wherever they go. She suggests that cars need trays as well as cupholders, but I think that's a bad idea. Eating while driving is really quite dangerous. It distracts the driver's attention and leads to accidents; therefore, people should wait to eat until they get home (p. 57).

"Human communication depends largely on signs in the form of written or spoken words, images, or gestures. These symbols are conscious and explicit representations of reality—of objects, actions, and concepts in the world around us. But there is another aspect of symbolism that is equally important though less explicit: the side that relates to our inner psychological and spiritual world. Within this inner world, a symbol can represent some deep intuitive wisdom that eludes direct expression."

—Fontana, D. (1993). *The Secret Language of Symbols*. San Francisco: Chronicle Books.

_____ 8. **Student version:** Symbols have two important functions. David Fontana says that they help humans communicate with another, and they also stand for the ideas and knowledge within us that are not always easy to express (pp. 9–10).

_____ 9. **Student version:** Symbols serve two purposes, according to David Fontana. They are, on the one hand, conscious and explicit representations of reality—of objects, actions, and concepts in the world around us. On the other hand, they can represent some deep intuitive wisdom that eludes direct expression (1993, pp. 9–10).

_____ 10. **Student version:** David Fontana (1993) says that symbols serve two important purposes. They function as signs that help us communicate with one another, and they also help us understand inner wisdom that is difficult to express. Fontana claims that this second purpose is more important than the first (pp. 9–10).

Answers: Summarizing, Paraphrasing & Quoting

1. b. a summary.

2. c. stealing.

3. b. giving a direct quotation

4. b. the author, title, and source of the original

5. a. the name of the writer and a reference to the source

6. Incorrect: the student writer used verbatim wording from the source, but did not surround them with quotation marks; incorrect source citation.

7. Correct: the citation information is correct. The student writer paraphrased the author and offered a personal, argumentative stance.

8. Correct: this brief summary is correctly cited and phrased.

9. Incorrect: the student writer used verbatim wording from the source, but did not surround them with quotation marks.

10. Incorrect: the student writer misinterprets the author's ideas. The author did not state that one symbol was more important than another.

Chapter Ten
Essential APA Format

Photo by Christina Morillo from Pexels.

Citing Your Resources

Whenever you write papers, you must include outside research from credible sources. You cannot rely on your personal opinions or beliefs about a topic, because your work must remain as objective as possible. The outside resources that you include within your paper must be properly documented according to an approved academic style guide. The most popular style guides include those from the *Modern Language Association* (MLA), *American Psychological Association* (APA), *The Chicago Manual of Style* (CMOS), and the *Turabian Style Guide*. These references are formatted according to one of these styles and cited in a bibliography at the end of your paper. A bibliography is the very last section of your research paper, thesis or dissertation that gives credit to previously published research on your topic. To avoid plagiarism, you must give credit for every source you summarize, paraphrase, or directly cite in your paper. This page is called a *Works Cited* (MLA), *References* (APA), or *Bibliography* (CMOS & Turabian).

What is APA Format?

Among academic style guides, APA is favored among the social sciences. It is also fast becoming the go-to guide for business departments and workplace writing. This guide is published by The American Psychological Association that is now in its 7th edition, which was released in October 2019. In the past, the APA guide targeted psychology professionals who conducted research and was not student-friendly. As a result, other academics and instructors attempted to offer a simplified version to assist students with their research writing. If you consult one of these unofficial guides, you must always double-check these resources against the actual APA guide for accuracy.

Sample APA References Page

References

Associated Press (2009). Black-white student achievement gap persists. Retrieved from MSNBC.com http://www.msnbc.msn.com/id/31911075/ns/us_news-education

Bloomquist, J. (2009). Class and categories: What role does socioeconomic status play in children's lexical and conceptual development? *Multilingua*, *28*(4), 327-353. doi:10.1515/mult.2009.015.

Carter, N., Hawkins, T., & Natesan, P. (2008). The Relationship between Verve and the Academic Achievement of African American Students in Reading and Mathematics in an Urban Middle School. *Educational Foundations*, 22(1-2), 29-46. Retrieved from ERIC database.

Chavous, T., Rivas-Drake, D., Smalls, C., Griffin, T., & Cogburn, C. (2008). Gender Matters, Too: The Influences of School Racial Discrimination and Racial Identity on Academic Engagement Outcomes Among African American Adolescents. *Developmental Psychology*, *44*(3), 637-654. doi:10.1037/0012-1649.44.3.637.

Common Reference Sources

When writing graduate research papers, you will include certain types of sources over and over again. Below is a short list of the most commonly used reference sources in graduate school writing. All of the citations follow APA 7th edition guidelines. Remember to verify the edition of APA format that your instructor or educational institution requires.

Book

Peck, M. S. (1998). *The road less traveled: a new psychology of love, traditional values, and spiritual growth*. Simon and Schuster.

Electronic Journal Article

Lawrence, A. (2011). Relationship Between Study Habits and Academic Achievement of Higher Secondary School Students. *Indian Journal of Applied Research, 4*(6), 143–145. https://doi.org/10.15373/2249555x/june2014/43

Magazine

Peterzell, J. (1990, April). Better late than never. *Time, 135*(17), 20–21.

Newspaper

Krugman, P. (2007, May). Fear of eating. *New York Times*, A1.

Website

Purdue Writing Lab. (2008). *Purdue OWL // Purdue Writing Lab*. Purdue Writing Lab. http://owl.english.purdue.edu/owl.

Web Article

Godoy, M., & Wood, D. (2020, May 30). *What Do Coronavirus Racial Disparities Look Like State By State?* NPR. https://www.npr.org/sections/health-shots/2020/05/30/865413079/what-do-coronavirus-racial-disparities-look-like-state-by-state.

Video Source

Muszynski, S. (2006). *Teen Pregnancy: What are the Consequences?* [DVD]. Sherborn, MA; Aquarius Health Care Media.

APA Format Knowledge Check

Directions: Circle the correct answer.

1. What element does not belong in an APA citation for a book?

   a. author

   b. date

   c. page numbers

2. You must italicize the name of a magazine article.

   a. true

   b. false

   c. not relevant

3. What is missing from the following citation for this newspaper article?

   Krugman, P. (May). Fear of eating. *New York Times*, A1.

   a. author

   b. year

   c. section

4. What element is absolutely mandatory for a website citation?

   a. web url link

   b. author

   c. article title

5. What is not required for a video source citation?

   a. title

   b. actors

   c. release date

Answers: 1. (c) 2. (a. true) 3. (b. year) 4. (a. web url link) 5. (b. actors)

Chapter Eleven
Online Research Skills

Photo by Vlada Karpovich from Pexels.

Conducting Online Research

In graduate school, you will be required to stretch your research skills beyond *Google* searches. Instead, you will rely on various academic databases to retrieve peer-reviewed articles and other scholarly materials. Generally, these databases are not open to the public and require a paid subscription from educational institutions. Therefore, it is important for you to become familiar with the digital library resources your school provides.

As a graduate student, your go-to resource for information should be your academic library. Although you can seek assistance from a reference librarian, you need to know how to effectively search for pertinent content that relates to your research topic. The following strategies presented as bullet points will help you develop the critical search skills needed to organize and outline your personal approach to conducting research online. As a review on how to get started, refer back to the *Basic Steps of the Research Process* section in Chapter 4 "Your Research Skills" in this book.

Five Steps to an Effective Search

1. **Make a Research Plan**

   Before you begin your research, it is a good idea to have a plan, so that you can stay focused and organized. Writing down questions that you need answered and general notes on what you need for your assignment will help you to manage your time wisely. Browse your academic library for helpful research tools, such as an assignment calendar.

2. **Select a Database**

   The number of databases you can access to support your research topic depends on your institution's subscriptions. Large colleges and universities tend to purchase the full range of available academic databases. However, community colleges and smaller institutions tend to limit their selections.

   Nonetheless, each database contains a unique collection of resources. Some collections contain journal articles tailored toward a specific field, and some contain more specialized resources like dissertations, reference books, and testing instruments.

3. **Select the Best Keywords**

   The words you use for searching are known as keywords. Databases find articles by matching the *exact* keywords you typed in the search boxes to the articles within the database that use those same words. A successful database search hinges on using a variety of relevant keywords related to your research topic.

4. **Build and Submit Your Search**

   Most databases provide either one search box for simple keywords and phrases (basic search) or multiple search boxes (advanced search). An advanced search is much more powerful and allows you more control over how the database finds your articles. Many research databases provide advanced search options, such as publication date, content type or discipline. See the illustration at the end of this chapter.

5. **Refine Your Search**

   If your search yields thousands of resources, that means your keywords are too broad. In this case, you will need to add limiters to your keywords. A manageable set of results generally retrieves 100-300 relevant articles. For example, if a basic database search for "distance education" generates 10,500 results, then you should try longer phrases like "distance education and minority students" to pull fewer, but pertinent sources.

Credible Research Tools

The following is a shortlist of the kind of research and productivity tools you should look for in your academic library or at your local public library.

RefWorks
Use this research management tool to collect, organize, and store citations from library databases and other resources in APA format.

Assignment Calculator
Manage your assignments by breaking the research and writing processes into discrete steps with specific deadlines. Assignment calculators estimate the time it will take to complete a courseroom assignment. The rate at which you progress will depend on many factors, such as your ability to manage your time.

Lib-Web-Cats at Libraries.org
A directory of libraries throughout the world. Also, access information from leading organizations such as the Association of Research Libraries.

National Network of Libraries of Medicine
Use this database to help you find local health libraries. *The National Library of Medicine* has over 4,500 member and affiliate libraries that provide health access to health science libraries and information centers.

WorldCat
Worldcat.org is a catalog of over 1 billion books and other materials held in libraries worldwide. Use your zip code to find an item in a library near you.

Public Online Libraries:

- **The WWW Virtual Library**
  www.vlib.org

- **The Digital Public Library of America**
  www.dp.la

- **The Electronic Library for Minnesota**
  www.elibrarymn.org

- **Internet Archive**
  www.archive.org

- **Library Spot**
  www.libraryspot.com

Advanced Internet Research Strategies

Use these strategies for general internet browser searches. In fact, try typing the example search phrases into the *Google* search box to see what appears. Remember, *Wikipedia* and similar sites are not credible research sources for graduate school writing.

- Use wildcards to broaden a search by adding an asterisk in place of an unknown term.
  Example: Holmes * Baker Street

- Use quotes to search for exact words and to prevent broader interpretation of a search term.
  Example: "distance learning strategies for teachers"

- Filter the results by excluding words or whole websites by adding a dash before terms you want to remove.
  Example: apple -computer -wikipedia.com

- Search within a specific website from within *Google* by limiting a search to one domain.
  Example: distance education site:usatoday.com

After submitting the searches above, I discovered…

My Notes:_____

_____

_____

Troubleshoot Common Search Problems

Inevitably, you will find broken links and missing resources while conducting online research. Over time, websites are reorganized and even renamed. This can break links to homepages, file downloads and other digital resources. These strategies can help you reroute your search and find the information you need.

- **Shorten the URL.** If a website has reorganized without redirecting a link, it may appear that a page is missing when it really just moved. One option you can try is to browse "upward" in a site to find a better path. Consider this example. If you are looking for a resource at **www.arhampton.com/classes/graduateresearchwriting** and the link is broken, try removing everything after the last / back slash, and use **www.arhampton.com/classes** instead. If that does not work, go to the root homepage **www.arhampton.com** as a starting point for a new search for the information that was moved.

- **Use another source.** If you find a broken link to an article that you want to read, try searching on *Google* for the article title or author's name. If the original source for an article has changed, searching for the exact title through another source or browser might locate that article.

- **Search within the webpage.** Quickly find items within a webpage by searching in the browser. Type **Control + F (Windows)** or **Command + F (Mac)** to bring up a search box and enter a keyword. This is particularly helpful for complex sites with many pages.

- **Resolve security warnings.** If receive a security alert while browsing a site, read the warning before proceeding. Click away from the site or take other necessary actions to clear the warning. Since many spam sites initiate false warnings, do not click on anything that looks suspicious or that suddenly pops up on your screen.

  A few common examples of security warnings include:

  - **"Information you have entered is to be sent over an unencrypted connection."** This means that you are browsing on a secure site, but are using a form that is not secured. Sometimes images on a secure page may be displayed from an unsecured connection. As long as you are not entering personal information, this is not generally a serious problem.

  - **"This connection is untrusted."** This is generally a warning that a website's security certificate is not valid or current. This can be a sign that the website is a security risk and should probably be avoided.

Advanced Search Box

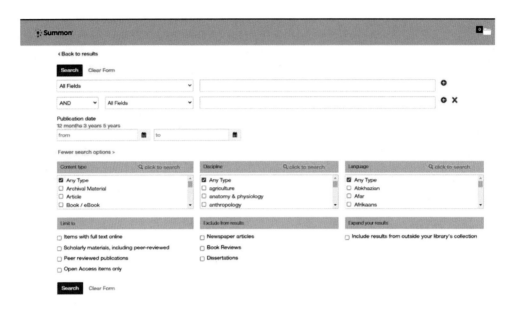

Search Strategy Worksheet

Before searching indexes and catalogs, you should clarify the information you are seeking by developing a search strategy. This worksheet presents an example of a four-step search strategy that was adapted from one developed by Humboldt State University.

Creating a Search Strategy

STEP 1: SUMMARIZE TOPIC

Clearly state your topic in one or two sentences. Be as specific as possible.

The affects of home schooling on K-12 students.

Example: I want to find information on how home schooling affects social development.

STEP 2: IDENTIFY CONCEPTS

Underline or number the main concepts represented in the topic summary completed above. Concepts are the different ideas which make up each unique search topic. Most topics can be broken down into two or three main concepts.

Example: I want to find information on how home schooling affects social development.

Keywords: home school, home schooling, social development

STEP 3: SELECT CONCEPT WORDS/PHRASES

In the *Your Search Topic* section below, create a list of words or phrases which describes each of your numbered concepts identified in Step 2. In making a list of keywords consider the following:

1. Use "free text" words and phrases likely to appear in the title. Try to think of appropriate synonyms or variant forms since a variety of words and phrases can be used to describe the same concept.

2. Use "controlled" words and phrases added to each reference in an index or catalog. These are useful for aggregating a concept described by several synonymous words. Use the thesaurus or indexing guide provided by the database you are searching for a list

of terms. Many databases have a thesaurus that lists their "controlled" words.

3. While developing keyword lists, consider possible hierarchical relationships within a particular concept. For example, with a taxonomic concept, are you only interested in locating research on a particular species or is a broader taxonomic classification also of interest; or for a geographic concept, are you only interested in a particular country or is the broader region also of interest?

4. Use word truncation. Examine each keyword to see if it can be truncated with a symbol (e.g., *, #, ?, +) to retrieve all variant forms after its "root" form, such as plurals. For example, *prevent** will retrieve *prevention, preventing, prevented,* or *prevents.* To find the correct truncation symbol, consult the help section in the database you will be using.

This list of keywords is dynamic. As you deepen your research, and as your personal knowledge increases, your list of appropriate keywords will become more concise and relevant to your topic.

Sample Search Topic:

Concept 1		Concept 2
home schooling	**and**	socialization **or** social development **or** social skills

Your Search Topic:

Concept 1	Concept 2	Concept 3
Public schools, K-12, elementary and secondary education	Socialization, social development, social skills	Academic ability, improved grades

STEP 4: CONNECT WORDS AND CONCEPTS

Use logical (Boolean) operators – **OR, AND, NOT** – to connect the words/phrases and concepts which you have listed in *Your Search Topic* above. Follow Steps A and B below.

Step A: Within each concept connect words/phrases with the **OR** operator. You can also broaden a search by specifying that any of the listed words can appear in the same concept or article by adding an asterisk.

Example #1: socialization **OR** social development **OR** social skill*

In addition, place parentheses before the first word and after the last word in each concept if you are using the **OR** operator. This will avoid computer processing confusion.

Step B: Connect different concepts with the **AND** or **NOT** operator.

Example #2: home schooling **AND** social development

NOT narrows a search by specifying that a word or concept must **not** appear in the same article. It is designed to eliminate unwanted words or concepts, but it might also eliminate relevant articles.

Example #3: home schooling **AND** social development **NOT** home instruction

YOUR BOOLEAN SEARCH COMBINATIONS:

- socialization **OR** social development **OR** social skill*
- home schooling **AND** social development
- home schooling **AND** social development **NOT** home instruction

Research Exercise

Directions: Identify each of the following statements as true or false by circling the letter of the correct answer.

1. *Wikipedia* is a credible research tool.

    a. True
    b. False

2. Facts and statistics from outside sources must be documented, but direct quotations do not have to be documented.

    a. True
    b. False

3. The author's last name is usually the first piece of information in a bibliography entry.

    a. True
    b. False

4. Information from outside sources is usually interesting, but does not help support a research paper's main points.

    a. True
    b. False

5. Careful documentation of information gathered from outside sources will help prevent plagiarism.

    a. True
    b. False

Answers: 1. false 2. false 3. true 4. false 5. true

Chapter Twelve
Understanding Plagiarism

Photo by Vlada Karpovich from Pexels.

What is Plagiarism?

Plagiarism is using someone else's words without giving them proper credit in your paper. Essentially, plagiarism is intentionally or unintentionally stealing another writer's work.

To avoid plagiarism, practice these golden rules:
1. Always provide a citation for words and ideas that are not your own.
2. Always include outside sources on your references page.
3. Always create new assignments for every class. Do not copy or repurpose work that you have already written and submitted for another class.

Remember, whenever you include outside sources in your papers, document those sources in your list of references, even for paraphrased ideas. Do not forget, and always keep accurate records of your references. Some doctoral dissertations have been publicly recalled for plagiarism over missing citations. Unfortunately, absent-mindedness can cost you when it comes to proper documentation.

Plagiarism Situations

Consider the two situations below and decide if plagiarism has been committed.

Scenario #1

Your friend had your current instructor last semester. She gives you one of her papers that received a "B+". You make a few changes and submit it.

Is this plagiarism?

Yes! Your friend created the original paper and already received a grade. Even if you make changes to the paper, you are still using someone's else's work and trying to pass it off as your own without giving them credit. In this situation, you have committed plagiarism.

Scenario #2

You find an article on the internet that says exactly what you would like to say in your paper. You copy a few sentences and forget to add a citation.

Is this plagiarism?

Yes! Although this is considered unintentional plagiarism, you can still be charged with plagiarism, because the proper citation does not appear in your paper.

Plagiarism Exercise

Directions: Identify each of the following statements as true or false by circling the letter of the correct answer.

1. The words *plagiarism* and *paraphrasing* mean the same thing.
    a. True
    b. False

2. A summary is always shorter than the original source.
    a. True
    b. False

3. An indirect quotation is always enclosed in quotation marks.
    a.   True
    b.   False

Directions: Below is a source followed by passages from student papers. If the student has summarized, directly quoted, or indirectly quoted the source correctly, **write "C" for "correct" on the blank**. If you believe the source is incorrectly summarized or plagiarized, **write "I" for "incorrect."**

> "Americans are rushing to get tucked, suctioned, tightened, and tweaked like never before. More than 8.7 million people underwent cosmetic surgery in 2003, up 33 percent from the year before, according to the American Society of Plastic Surgeons. No longer a privilege of society wives and aging starlets, cosmetic surgery has gone mainstream, available to almost anyone with a credit card and some vacation time."
>
> —Shute, Nancy. "Makeover Nation." *U.S. News & World Report* 31 May 2004: 52.

_____ 4. **Student version:** Over the past several years, the number of people getting cosmetic surgery has dramatically increased. As Nancy Shute puts it, "Americans are rushing to get tucked, suctioned, tightened, and tweaked like never before" (2004, p. 52).

_____ 5. **Student version:** In America, having cosmetic surgery has become widely accepted. Over 8.7 million people went under the knife in 2003, a 33 percent increase from the year before. And it's not just "society wives and aging starlets" who are paying to change their looks, but all kinds of people (p. 52).

Answers: Plagiarism Exercise

1. The words *plagiarism* and *paraphrasing* mean the same thing.
    a. True
    <u>b. False</u>

2. A summary is always shorter than the original source.
    <u>a. True</u>
    b. False

3. An indirect quotation is always enclosed in quotation marks.
    a. True
    b. <u>False</u>

> "Americans are rushing to get tucked, suctioned, tightened, and tweaked like never before. More than 8.7 million people underwent cosmetic surgery in 2003, up 33 percent from the year before, according to the American Society of Plastic Surgeons. No longer a privilege of society wives and aging starlets, cosmetic surgery has gone mainstream, available to almost anyone with a credit card and some vacation time."

> —Shute, Nancy. "Makeover Nation." *U.S. News & World Report* 31 May 2004: 52.

<u>(C) Correct</u> 4. **Student version:** Over the past several years, the number of people getting cosmetic surgery has dramatically increased. As Nancy Shute puts it, "Americans are rushing to get tucked, suctioned, tightened, and tweaked like never before" (2004, p. 52).

<u>(I) Incorrect</u> 5. **Student version:** In America, having cosmetic surgery has become widely accepted. Over 8.7 million people went under the knife in 2003, a 33 percent increase from the year before. And it's not just "society wives and aging starlets" who are paying to change their looks, but all kinds of people (p. 52).

Chapter Thirteen
Evaluating Sources

Photo by Burst from Pexels.

Evaluating Sources

As you find sources for your research projects, be sure to read the abstract, introduction and conclusion before reading the whole thing to determine its relevancy. After getting a sense of the information presented in the source, ask yourself the following questions:

- Who is the author? An expert, academic or researcher? What are the author's qualifications?

- Consider the date of the publication. Is the publication recent (within the last 10 years) or older? Is the information still relevant to your discipline?

- Consider the audience. Was the article written for academic peers or a general audience?

- Look at the bibliography or reference page. What other works did the author reference to support their ideas?

- Are any of the citations in the bibliography helpful to your research?

Critical Analysis of a Source

- Determine the facts, arguments, and points of view expressed in the source.

- Did the author offer new findings?

- Is there clear evidence to support each main point?

- Is the source reliable, accurate, and balanced?

- Is the research methodology flawed or solid?

- Is the source free of personal bias?

- What is the significance of the article?

- How does it contribute to past and current research?

- What are its flaws, limitations, strengths or assumptions?

Key Points for Evaluating Sources

- Be selective in choosing outside research for your projects.
- Do not assume that a published work is completely accurate.
- Choose research that directly relates to and supports your own ideas about the topic.

After reading this section, I now understand…

My Notes:_____

_____

_____

Thinking Critically About Source Quality

Based on a checklist developed by Capella University, the questions below will help you determine if a source is credible. If your instructor allows non-scholarly sources, such as trade publications or magazine articles, choose sources that resemble scholarly articles in regard to evidence, audience, and content.

For example, although *Psychology Today* is a long-running magazine and not a scholarly journal, it features articles written by esteemed professionals in that discipline.

Remember: Nearly every library search tool has an option to check a box that says "scholarly/peer-reviewed." This option eliminates non-academic results such as magazines and newspapers. Refining your search in this way saves time by only retrieving results from peer-reviewed journals.

WHERE WAS THE SOURCE PUBLISHED, POSTED OR PRESENTED?

- Is the publisher well regarded? What evidence do you have to trust this publisher?
- Look at the publisher's website. What else do they publish?
- Is this source cited in other articles or used in your course readings?
- Is it on a university department, government agency, or professional organization's website?
- Does the website end in .org, .edu or .gov? As a rule, try to avoid websites ending in .com.
- Was it presented at an academic or professional conference?

WHAT ARE THE AUTHOR'S CREDENTIALS?

- Is the author a researcher in this field? What are the author's professional affiliations?
- Search for the author's website in a search engine. Where do they work and what is their education?
- What other things have been written by this author? Anything in peer-reviewed journals?
- What do you know about the author's reputation in the field?
- Is there anything to indicate he/she might have a bias to be aware of?

DOES THE PAPER USE QUALITY SOURCES AND EVIDENCE?

- What sources did the author use as evidence? Is there a long bibliography?
- Does it report on original or derivative research? (Is it a primary, secondary, or tertiary source?)
- Does it discuss current theories and use methodologies from your field?
- Is data analyzed correctly?
- Does it use the language of the discipline?

WHAT DO OTHER SCHOLARS SAY ABOUT THIS SOURCE?

- If the source is a book, are there reviews of it?
- Have other scholars used materials from the same source in their research?
- Are there similar arguments, theories, or ideas circulating in the peer-reviewed literature?

WHO IS THE AUDIENCE FOR THIS SOURCE?

- Is it intended for other scholars?
- Does it contain practical information that is more useful for a person working in the field?
- Is it educational and written for students?

Knowledge Check

1. Select the important aspect(s) to keep in mind when evaluating resources:

   a) Authority
   b) Timeliness
   c) Credibility
   d) All of these answers are correct

2. When selecting materials to use for your assignments, you should....

   a) Use anything from an academic library
   b) Evaluate the author and source using appropriate criteria
   c) Use whatever you can find until you get enough sources
   d) Stick to scholarly materials which do not need to be evaluated

Answers: 1. d 2. b

CARS Evaluation Checklist

Based on an article written by Robert Harris called, "Evaluating Internet Research Sources," the **CARS Checklist** is designed to assist researchers in evaluating sources. **CARS** stands for **Credibility, Accuracy, Reasonableness and Support.** Most sources will never meet every single criterion on this list. However, applying these criteria to potential resources for your papers allows you to separate high-quality information from fake news as you conduct your research.

Credibility

Because people have always made important decisions based on information, evidence of authenticity has always been important. **Credibility** is a measure of the authenticity or reliability of a source of information. To determine credibility, you might ask: *Why should I believe this source over another? How does the author know this information? What makes this source believable or not?*

Indicators of credibility:

An author's credentials consist of their training and education in a particular academic field of study. Look for the author's degree, title or position of employment. Does the author provide contact information (email or snail mail address, phone number)? If the source of the information is an organization or group, ask yourself if it is a respected body (e.g., the Mayo Clinic or the American Dental Association).

Evidence of quality control—most scholarly information passes through a process of **peer review**, whereby several experts within that field of study review the author's writings to ensure that their conclusions are valid and in keeping with current knowledge in the field. Journals of this type are known as **academic, scholarly, peer-reviewed** or **refereed** publications, and they are available both online and in print formats.

Information presented on organizational websites is also generally peer-reviewed, since it is issued in the name of an organization like the American Psychological Association (APA), for example.

Indicators of a possible lack of credibility:

- Anonymity (no author listed)—why is the author hiding?

- A lack of quality control (see explanation above).

- Poor graphic or visual presentation. Credible authors/websites present their information in a well-organized and professional manner. A poorly designed website can be an indicator that the information is less than credible.

- Bad grammar or misspelled words. Educated people use grammar fairly well and regularly proofread their work for errors. An occasional error is not unusual, but more than two or three spelling or grammar errors is cause for caution at least. Whether the errors resulted from carelessness or ignorance, neither puts the information or the writer in a favorable light.

Accuracy

The goal of the accuracy test is to ensure that the information is actually correct, meaning up-to-date, detailed, exact, and comprehensive. Keep in mind that something that was true twenty years ago may no longer be true today. This is especially true in fast-changing fields, like medicine, healthcare and technology. On the other hand, a reputable source might be current, but the information is only partial and not the full story. Being knowledgeable of the subject matter enables you to make an informed judgment as to a source's accuracy.

Indicators of accuracy:
- In many disciplines (e.g., the sciences, medicine, technology), **timeliness** is a very important measure of the relevance of scholarly information, and therefore, its accuracy, since new discoveries are constantly being created and previously known 'facts' about a subject are constantly changing. Therefore, you need to note the publication date of the information you find, and decide whether it is still of value. As a rule, use sources published within the last ten years.

  With that being said, old information is not necessarily bad. Nineteenth-century American history books or literary anthologies can still be highly educational when compared with what is being written or anthologized now. Some work is timeless, such as the philosophical works of Aristotle and Plato. In most cases, however, you will limit your research to the most accurate and up-to-date information you can find.

- Another indicator of accuracy is **comprehensiveness**. The ideal article or website presents a thorough discussion of the subject, as opposed to only "touching on the highlights." Since no single piece of information can truly offer a complete story, you must consult multiple sources in a variety of different formats, such as books, scholarly journal articles, or material from online databases.

- Finally, **lack of personal bias** can signal accuracy. By addressing all sides of an issue, the author ensures a complete and objective treatment of the topic. Although biased information is not completely useless, the slanted perspective must be taken into consideration when assessing its pertinence to your research.

Indicators of a possible lack of accuracy:

- A source that deliberately leaves out important facts, qualifications, consequences or alternatives may be misleading or even intentionally deceptive.

- Vague or sweeping generalizations as opposed to exact facts and figures.

- No date on the document or a very old date on a document, particularly one containing time-sensitive information.

- A very one-sided view that does not acknowledge or address opposing views. Beware; information pretending to be objective, but possessing a hidden agenda or hidden bias inundates the information centers of our culture.

Reasonableness

Reasonable information is fair, objective, moderate, and consistent.

Indicators of reasonableness:

- In regards to **fairness**, look for a balanced and well-reasoned argument. The tone of an academic resource should be factual and thoughtful. A reasonable source presents information objectively without attempting to rile your emotions. When browsing resources outside of an academic database, be especially cautious of highly incendiary writing.

- Pure **objectivity** is almost impossible to find, but a good writer should eliminate obvious biases. Be aware that some individuals, organizations, and higher education institutions are unabashedly biased, so be wary of skewed perspectives or politically-distorted work.

- Another indicator—**moderateness**—assesses the probability or likelihood of a writer's assertions. If you find claims that are surprising or difficult to believe or that sharply deviate from your own knowledge and experience, look for other peer-reviewed sources that have been properly vetted. However, do not automatically reject a claim or a source simply because it is astonishing. Just be extra careful when checking it out.

- Look for **consistency**. The facts and findings in an article (or website) should not contradict themselves in other parts of the same article (or website). Sometimes, when writers spin falsehoods or distort the truth, inconsistencies arise.

Indicators of a possible lack of reasonableness:

- A shrill or overly aggressive tone on the part of the author (e.g., referring to opponents as "stupid jerks" or belittling findings. Writing that is slanted toward ego, personal bias or self-interests often indicates a lack of reasonableness.

- Overclaims—when the language is too grandiose or hyperbolic. These sorts of statements are seldomly supported with objective evidence.

- Sweeping generalizations, such as *"It is obvious to everyone that...".*

- Data that contradicts itself.

- Conflicts of interest. How trustworthy is a report that claims dairy is essential to good health from a producer of high-end cheese products?

Support

Most information presented in an article comes from other sources. So, you need to ask yourself: *Where did this information come from? What sources did the author use? Is there a bibliography or other source documentation? How does the writer know this?* It is especially important that statistical information be documented. Authors strengthen their credibility by properly citing their sources.

Indicators of support:

- **Corroboration.** Do other sources agree with the information in this source? Corroboration or confirmability is an important test. While researching your topic, it is a good idea to triangulate your data, which means to find at least three sources that agree with each other. If your sources do not agree, you should do further research to find out the range of opinions or disagreements within the field before drawing your own conclusions.

- **External consistency.** Does the source agree or harmonize with other sources, or does it conflict, exaggerate or distort? If a source presents faulty interpretations of subject matter that is widely accepted in the field, any new information it provides might be untrustworthy.

- The claims made in the writer's argument are supported by facts or figures from clearly noted sources.

- Proper documentation and citation. A bibliography or list of references appears at the end of the article (or website), for example.

Indicators of a possible lack of support:

- Numbers or statistics are presented without an identifiable source.

- Absence of source documentation when the discussion clearly calls for such documentation.

- No other sources present the same information or acknowledge that the author's claims exist, which suggests a lack of corroboration.

- The author's claims are not supported with sufficient evidence.

1. After reading this section, I think I need to…

2. Now, I understand how to…

Fact or Opinion Exercise

Directions: Read each statement and indicate whether it is a fact or opinion. Explain your answer. Search the internet if you are unsure of a response.

1. Michael Jordan has a career average of 30.4 points per game.

   Fact or Opinion

   Explain: _____

2. George Washington was the first President of the United States under the Constitution.

   Fact or Opinion

   Explain: _____

3. There seems to be too much standardized testing in public schools.

   Fact or Opinion

   Explain: _____

4. Vegetarians are healthier than people who eat meat.

   Fact or Opinion

   Explain: _____

5. Cell phones emit radiation that can cause brain cancer.

   Fact or Opinion

   Explain: _____

6. Diamonds are the hardest substance on Earth.

   Fact or Opinion

   Explain: _____

7. Popular music today is not as good as it was in the past.

   Fact or Opinion

   Explain: _____

Chapter Fourteen
Scholarly Peer–Reviewed Articles

Photo by Trent Erwin from Unsplash.

What is Scholarly Writing?

Scholarly writing is mostly associated with faculty or graduate students who engage in research and document their findings in articles that are published by an academic institution or a professional organization. For example, an English instructor who has written about the feminist themes in Zora Neale Hurston's fiction might submit her work to a notable literary feminist journal. If the editors agree that her work offers an interesting perspective and adds to the discussion of feminism, then her article gets published. The instructor is proud and highly esteemed, because her work passed a stringent peer-review process before being accepted for publication. In a nutshell, this is what is meant by scholarly writing and peer-reviewed articles. Peer-review is the process by which an author's fellow faculty and other recognized researchers in the field, read and evaluate a paper (article) submitted for publication and recommend whether the paper should be published, revised, or rejected. Peer-review is a widely accepted indicator of quality scholarship in a discipline or field, because articles accepted for publication through a peer-review process have met the discipline's standards of expertise.

What are Peer-Reviewed Articles?

Quite simply, peer-reviewed articles—as previously described—are published in scholarly journals that are found through a library's academic databases. Peer-reviewed (also called *refereed*) journals only publish scholarly articles that have passed through this review process.

In academic publishing, the goal of peer-review is to assess the quality of articles submitted for publication in a scholarly journal. Before an article is deemed appropriate for publication in a peer-reviewed journal, it must undergo the following process:

- The author of the article must submit it to the journal editor who forwards the article to experts in the field. Because the reviewers specialize in the same scholarly area as the author, they are considered the author's peers, hence the phrase "peer-review".

- These impartial reviewers are charged with carefully evaluating the quality of the submitted manuscript.

- The peer reviewers check the manuscript for accuracy and assess the validity of its research methodology and procedures.

- If appropriate, they suggest revisions. If they find the article lacking in scholarly validity and rigor, they reject the submission.

Because a scholarly journal will not publish articles that fail to meet the standards established by a given discipline, peer-reviewed articles accepted for publication exemplify the best research practices in a field.

There are several types of articles found in peer-reviewed journals:
- **Original research articles:** Offer fresh perspectives on established research, concepts or theories and the science behind the results
- **Case studies:** Report on unique occurrences that can contribute to the existing knowledge in a field of study
- **Literature reviews or review articles:** Provide an overview of multiple articles in a certain field
- **Correction or retraction articles:** Update the findings of a study or refute previously published findings
- **Commentary articles and editorials:** Provide opinions and personal viewpoints (bias) from experts in the field, often about controversial and current topics
- **Media and book reviews**: Provide reviews of recent scholarly books, websites or reports (not typically considered "articles" to use in an academic paper)

Features of a Scholarly Article

Most scholarly, peer-reviewed articles have a similar organizational pattern that generally includes the following:

Date Published:	• The date when the article was published.
Article Title:	• The title of the article.
Author(s) and Author Affiliation:	• The author or authors of the article and their academic or corporate institution.
Abstract:	• Brief, comprehensive summary of the article that helps determine if the article is relevant.
Introduction & Background:	• States the reason for the research and gives background information about the issue being studied; might also include a literature review of the topic.
Methodology:	• Describes the population being studied, the methods used to gather the data, and the methods used to analyze the data.
Results:	• Summarizes the results and findings using text, tables, charts and graphs.
Discussion:	• Analyzes results; explains their significance and discusses further research.
Reference:	• A bibliography or list of the publications that were cited to support the research.

Scholarly Source Quiz

1. What kind of sources constitute peer-reviewed research?
   a) Articles where peers review articles after they are published
   b) Scholarly journals with rigorous publication review requirements
   c) Publications that have subscribers with a certain expertise
   d) Books, articles or websites or anything by scholars in the field

2. If you are searching for scholarly articles, books or trade publications based on a topic, where should you do the majority of your searching?
   a) An open web search engine like Google
   b) Library collections and databases
   c) Government websites
   d) Public libraries

3. Which of the following are features of scholarly or peer-reviewed articles? Read each choice carefully.
   a) Generally, longer than five pages
   b) Often lists the age, race, and gender of its authors
   c) Includes lots of scholarly citations
   d) Includes a Methodology, Discussion, and Results

4. You are assigned the topic of "learning theories," but you do not know where to start. Where can you go to find more contextual information or examples regarding this topic? Read each option carefully to find the best fit.

   a) Books, library databases, credible websites, or course readings
   b) Primarily books, especially textbooks
   c) Primarily periodicals outside of the library
   d) Only scholarly publications in the library's reference databases

Answers: 1. (b)   2. (b)   3. (d)   4. (a)

The Ivory Tower Ain't No Crystal Stair: Essentializing the Experiences of the Black Female Scholar

Ashan R. Hampton

Department of English, Morehouse College

May 29, 2000

The Ivory Tower Ain't No Crystal Stair: Essentializing the Experiences of the Black Female Scholar

During the summer of my first year of teaching, I was invited to instruct a Composition II course at Pulaski Technical College in North Little Rock, Arkansas. On the first day of class, I arrived a bit early and sat in one of the student desks to observe the demeanor of those who entered the room and to hear snatches of conversation that might reveal their expectations or attitudes about the course. I knew that those who had arrived early enough to see me sitting there would realize my trickery in posing as a student, as they watched me blithely move toward the front of the room to begin class.

As the students continued to file in, I became more and more aware of my discomfort and anticipation to see another female, or an African-American, or better yet, an African-American female like myself. With the exception of a handful of women, only two of whom were Black, I found myself standing in front of a class composed predominately of white males. They varied in age, but most wore baseball caps, fraternity paraphernalia, cowboy boots or tennis shoes. They all seemed to possess the ruddiness and features of those shaped and honed by the forces of rural America. The rounded *Skoal* imprints on many of their behind pockets, signified their paucity of experience and contact with other ethnicities.

Although class progressed rather well, without major incident, whenever a male student began to challenge my instruction, I could not figure out if my gender or race had begotten the student's defensive posture.

Upon reflection of that experience, I concluded that a little of both had

tapped segments of his ego that he had genuinely tried to restrain. When

male hegemony laced with racial prejudice did manifest themselves in a

public, intellectual challenge, my femaleness and my Blackness were

momentarily cacophonous to the socialization of gender and class he had

been subjected to in *Small-Town U.S.A.*

This binary mode of experience that being both female and Black

engenders has been much debated, negated and theorized; however, in the

case of W.E.B. DuBois and his concept of "double-consciousness," the

theoretical begins to meet the experiential when thinking of the grab bag of

misogynist attitudes and racial stereotypes the Black female scholar must

contend with. Black women still have to navigate amid their peculiar

position of being both woman and Black, where both are, to some degree,

considered inferior. Unfortunately, regardless of how progressive we think

the academy has become, the specters of race and gender continue to veil,

and quite often diminish the intellectual merit of the Black female scholar's

instruction and scholarship.

The concept of "double-consciousness" that DuBois introduced,

sought to reveal and fuse the dual identity of Blacks of both African and

American descent. When gender is added to complete this triad of disjunctive experience, doing so all the more intensifies the alienation often felt by the African-American female, who cannot readily resolve the concomitance of privilege and disdain her experience evokes.

In her essay, *Visible Woman; or, A Semester Among the Great Books*, professor Eileen Julien writes of her experience teaching a graduate course entitled, *Western Literary Traditions after 1500* to an all white class. She asserts that her racial identity, or the stigma attached to it, generated poor student reviews, and caused her reading of the material to be questioned. Julien also takes the opportunity to make several provocative and bold assertions about the westernization of the literary canon, and the extent to which her experience, knowledge and pedagogy were essentialized.

Many African-American scholars, not just women, must at some point answer to the accusations of ideology, and the Black scholar's ability to read and teach non-Black texts in a non-tendentious, non-discriminatory manner. Julien writes of her experience with this issue, "The students apparently had been forewarned by another colleague—so I was told later by someone in the class—that Professor Julien's course would probably be "ideological." Black, most of them saw quite clearly, comes with baggage. White of course, comes with none (227)."

The assumption here is that Blackness prohibits a scholar from giving an authentic, intellectual reading of the classical canons of literature, which were dominated by the authorship of white males who often held very conservative, prejudicial ideas on race and gender. The implicit idea behind the colleague's comments about ideology is that the course might be tainted by *'Black stuff'*—Black philosophy, Black ideas—that will distort the hallowed literary objectives of our great literary masters. In this sense, Black ideas and thoughts are seen as subversive as opposed to mainstream, and the construct of Blackness has somehow become an obscurant to pure intellectual thought and exchange. Interestingly enough, the term "ideological" seems to become a bad word when used to refer to the framework of ideas that Blacks supposedly operate from. This term then connotes inferiority, and questions the authority of Blacks to teach European texts. Herein lies the argument of essentialism.

When speaking of Black women within academe, the essentialist and constructionist schools of thought cease to be polarized, but find some common ground. Black women are born naturally and biologically as women, but 'Blackness' is very much a social construction forced upon those of us who have been determined to be so. In academe, essentialism is voiced in questions such as, "Must one be Black in order to create or understand Black literature?" That is to say, "Is there something inherent, or immutable, 'essential,' about a Black person that would give him or her the authority to speak of Blackness better than an 'other,' to the point that no one else can occupy that space?"

In light of the essentialist and constructionist arguments, Black women are born female, but the assertion that society has made them both Black and female is certainly a provocative one. Therefore, the social construct of blackness cannot be separated from the biological idea of woman when attempting to articulate the essence of Black women's experiences within and outside of academe. Unfortunately, as the illustrations cited in this paper illustrate, Black women will inevitably deal with society's working definitions of woman and blackness within academe, where some innocently believe that intellectual and academic pursuits are homogenizing forces that subordinate concerns of race and gender.

Race is so inextricably bound to the American concept of self that to separate one from the other would be to rip an extremity from the body. We are painfully bound by not only our genetic composition, but also the external influences of people places, and things that have constituted the manner in which we have been socialized to identify ourselves. Unfortunately, most Americans, whether born here or not, have been taught to think and behave in terms of Black and white racial identity. These ideas have been indoctrinated and sustained in our attitudes and psyche, and have fostered the stereotype of inferiority that women and Blacks have been

branded with, and Black women doubly so.

In *The Black Notebooks*, Toi Derricotte shares a similar situation

with a white student, in which both of their frustrations with the issue of

race were publicly expressed:

> A few weeks ago, I got angry at a student in one of my creative
>
> writing classes who complained that I was talking too much about
>
> race. She said there were people in the class who were tired of hearing
>
> about it. I have heard that complaint from white students before, and
>
> in the past, I have been patient, tried to listen and clarify my purposes
>
> in a more tolerant manner. This time, however, I found myself tired
>
> and lashing out. "If you don't like it, you don't have to stay." She
>
> looked devastated. (119)

Derricotte's narrative affirms the fact that when students and faculty

enter the classroom, they do not cease to be or to think according to their

racial identities. "Institutions cannot discount the power of race and other

such categories, their centrality and tenacity in ways of reading within and

beyond the classroom" (Julien 233). Race very much informs the ideas and

the scholarship of those within academe and to deny this is to deprive the

academy of a rich and diverse body of knowledge. Therefore, to be Black

and to think accordingly is not necessarily a bad thing.

However, Diana Fuss, in the chapter of her book, *Essentially Speaking* called "Essentialism in the Classroom," seems to diminish the attachment of racial identity to the notion of person, and the subsequent experiences that arise from this confluence when she writes, "It is certainly true that there is no such thing as "the female experience" or "the Black experience" or "the Jewish experience"…And it seems likely that simply being a woman, or a Black, or a Jew (as if "being" were ever simple) is not enough to qualify one as an official spokesperson for an entire community" (117). I cannot agree with this statement when it is so obvious to me that many scholars and major players of feminist movements who are held in high esteem, have established very lucrative careers based upon their 'expertise' on women's issues, Black history, Black thought, and otherwise living life on the peripheries of the American experience.

With regard to authority and experience within the scholarship of Black women, bell hooks writes in her book, *Remembered Rapture: The Writer at Work*, "Black women grapple continually with the suspicions of a larger literary world that is still not confident we are serious thinkers and writers" (xii-xiii). The idea that being Black and female somehow undermines the intellectual acumen of the Black woman is evident within this statement. It also suggests that Black women cannot expand themselves enough to speak beyond Blackness and gender.

Psychologically, we are bound and governed by our experiences. They dictate who we are, how we act and what we say. As Fuss states, "…personal identity metamorphoses into knowledge. Who we are becomes what we know; ontology shades into epistemology" (113). Essentially, we can only truly speak of what we know, thus the experience and voice of Black women must be honored and esteemed as intellectually challenging and valid.

Patricia Hill-Collins, in the article titled, "What's In A Name? Womanism, Black Feminism and Beyond," acknowledges the emergence and frequency of the Black female's voice in academia, but balances this perception of acceptance by reminding the reader of the limited physical presence of Black women in higher education:

> Black women appear to have a voice, and with this new-found voice comes a series of concerns. For example, we must be attentive to the seductive absorption of black women's voices in classrooms of higher education where black women's texts are still much more welcomed than black women ourselves. Giving the illusion of change, this strategy of symbolic inclusion masks how the everyday institutional policies and arrangements that suppress and

exclude African Americans as a collectivity remain virtually

untouched. (Collins 9)

It seems that the fascination with identity politics has created a space for the

scholarship of Black women to be duly acknowledged in discussions on

race, class, gender and sexuality; however, the privilege and disdain that

accompany the racialization of the black female body make their ideas

welcome in discussions of diversity, but the idea of the black female body in

the classroom is still immured by notions of race and gender.

The scholarship of Black women is often informed by personal

experiences related to the duality of identity that race and gender create.

Therefore, the scholarship does not only constitute pedantic words on paper,

but moves beyond text to involve readers in the experiences that have

engendered the writing of the scholarship. The connotation of inferiority of

texts written by Black scholars must be removed in order for Black

women's works and thoughts to cease to be 'special,' and accordingly

relegated to special topics courses or special issues of journals.

When applied to the attitudes and stereotypes Black women in

majority situations must contend with within the academy, which are often

steeped in essentialist and racist ideologies, it becomes evident that *"the*

ivory tower ain't no crystal stair." This statement, which has been adapted

from a line in Langston Hughes' poem, *Mother to Son*, refers to the peculiar and sometimes uncomfortable position Black female scholars are placed in

when they are favored and esteemed because of their racial identity, yet are

stealthily, intellectually subordinated, and otherwise subject to having their

authority and ability to function well at a majority institution undermined.

In conclusion, as we usher in a new millennium, old notions about

higher learning, pedagogy, scholarship, and the influences of race and

gender within academia, must change in order to understand and appreciate

the new breed of Black female scholar that generation-x has created. She is

coming with sister girl attitude, the rhythms of hip-hop music bouncing in

her head, and a proficiency in slang and academic jargon, all of which

constitute the intellectual panoply that will enable her to breathe new life

into old subjects in such a way that will force the old academic guard to

reconsider current expectations and evaluations of scholarship.

Until then, many Black female scholars will hide the scars of their

old war wounds they received during one or more situations where their

personage, gender and intellectual abilities were publicly challenged and

questioned, particularly at institutions or in situations where the presence of

Blacks was minimal to none. The outrage and silence that accrue when fear

prohibits many from vocalizing these frustrations have become

characteristic of the experiences of Black women who have to some extent

tolerated overt and or covert instances of racial mistreatment. The process of dialectically essentializing the experiences of black women in academe ultimately means acknowledging race and gender inequities as the core of those experiences.

The future success of Black female scholars therefore hinges upon taking a parallax view of race and gender, and the validity of the experiences both of these constructs produce, so that it becomes acceptable for them to authorize and inform pedagogical concerns, as well as scholarship.

Works Cited

Derricotte, Toi. <u>The Black Notebooks: An Interior Journey</u>. New York:

    WW Norton, 1997.

Fuss, Diana. <u>Essentially Speaking: Feminism, Nature and Difference</u>.

    New York: Routledge, 1989.

Hill-Collins, Patricia. "What's In a Name? Womanism, Black Feminism

    and Beyond." <u>Black Scholar</u> 26.1 (Winter/ Spring 1996): 9-18.

hooks, bell. <u>Remembered Rapture: The Writer at Work</u>. New York:

    Henry Holt & Co., 1999.

Julien, Eileen. "Visible Woman: or a Semester Among the Great Books."

    Professions (Fall/Winter 1999): 225-235.

Chapter Fifteen
Parts of a Research Paper

Photo by Tom Rogerson from Unsplash.

Essential Sections of Graduate Research Papers

Ultimately, your research topic and academic formatting style depend on your discipline and your degree level. Master's degree work might require a bit less complexity or sophistication than a doctoral dissertation. History majors prefer APA Style while English department scholars favor the MLA format. Nevertheless, there are certain elements of graduate writing that are common to all disciplines.

Regardless of your field of study, all graduate students must know how to successfully fashion an abstract, annotated bibliography, bibliography, and literature review.

After a brief description of each section, this chapter ends with an example of a full APA graduate research paper that illustrates how each part operates within the whole.

Abstract

- An abstract is a brief overview of the main points, recommendations and conclusions of your research.

- An abstract should summarize the entire research report without using quotes from the actual report.

- The abstract is also called an executive summary, depending on academic style format and is generally one paragraph between 5-7 or 10-15 sentences, but no longer than one page.

- Remember, an abstract is a synopsis of the body of your report, including the introduction, main points, findings, recommendations and conclusions.

- People should understand your research even without reading the entire paper.

Sample Abstract

The achievement gap among African American students and other ethnicities has been a long source of perplexity, embarrassment and exasperation among American educators. Although much has been researched and written about the unique learning styles of African American students, their socioeconomic and intellectual challenges, little statistical progress has been demonstrated in closing this achievement gap. In fact, African American students tend to drop out of high school in alarmingly disproportionate rates compared to other ethnic groups, particularly African American males. Considering the increasing need for educated citizens to meet the high technological demands of industry and daily living in a global, 21st century society, the low academic achievement of one ethnic group is simultaneously intriguing and problematic. If African American students enter public schools at an academic disadvantage in kindergarten, the very beginning of their academic careers, how then can they successfully matriculate through curricula that do not serve them at every grade level toward graduation to become productive American citizens? Since no significant demonstrable progress toward ameliorating this problem of low achievement among black students is evident, according to national statistics, does this indicate a sense of resignation among educators to continue searching for solutions?

Keywords: academic achievement, achievement gap, social learning theory, collaborative learning, learning styles

Annotated Bibliography

- An annotated bibliography is an alphabetical list of your research citations.

- First, each entry includes a brief summary of the main points of the article.

- After the summary, you might be asked to briefly comment on the value of the source.

- Additionally, you might need to briefly comment on how the source relates to your research project.

- Basically, an annotated bibliography summarizes and assesses the value of your sources.

- The annotated bibliography can be submitted as a standalone assignment, or attached to the end of your research paper.

Sample Annotated Bibliography Entry (APA 7th)

No Commentary or Analysis

Clement, A. J., & Lidsky, A. J. (2011). The danger of history slipping away: The heritage campus and HBCUs. *Planning for Higher Education, 39*(3), 149-158.

The authors argue that HBCUs are in danger of closing its doors due to poor maintenance and insufficient funds to make necessary repairs, in addition to other social and economic factors that typically affect these institutions.

After reading this section, I understand...

Bibliography

Depending on your academic writing style guide, the *Bibliography* (CMOS) is also called a *References* (APA) or *Works Cited* (MLA) page. It is the same as an annotated bibliography without the summaries or commentary/analysis. The bibliography is the last page or the last section of a research paper that contains an alphabetical listing of all the outside resources included in the body of the paper. Sources not directly cited or paraphrased should be excluded from the list. Overall, the purpose of a bibliography is to allow readers to track down your sources for their own purposes.

As a general rule, the sources on a bibliography should have been published within the last 10 years. Anything older than that is dated, and should only be used under exceptional circumstances. While developing your bibliography, consult your style guide for instructions on how to format your sources.

Here are some key points to remember about your bibliography:

- People will actually read through your references and some might even look them up out of curiosity, necessity or sheer pettiness.

- In-text parenthetical citations must match the bibliography. Whatever you cite in the body of your paper must be fully and properly documented in the bibliography.

- Some readers, especially in the academic community, will assess the quality of your work based on the authors you cite. So, make sure to incorporate the works of prominent or seminal scholars in your field.

Sample Bibliography Entry (MLA 8th)

Dean, Jodi. *Democracy and Other Neoliberal Fantasies: Communicative Capitalism and Left Politics*. Duke University Press, 2009.

(APA 7th)

Dean, J. (2009). *Democracy and other neoliberal fantasies: communicative capitalism and left politics*. Duke University Press.

(Chicago Manual of Style)

Dean, Jodi. *Democracy and Other Neoliberal Fantasies: Communicative Capitalism and Left Politics*. Duke University Press, 2009.

Literature Review

- A **literature review** is a comprehensive summary of previous research on a topic.
- A **literature review** surveys scholarly articles, books and other authoritative sources that relate to a particular area of research.

- A **literature review** objectively summarizes and evaluates the published research of authors who have written about the topic you are now researching.

- Before you begin drafting a master's thesis or dissertation, you must conduct a literature review to see what has already been written about your topic.

- As a researcher yourself, you will add your own perspective to the body of knowledge that has already been published on your topic.

Purposes of a Literature Review

- Identify seminal works and scholars in the field.

- Acknowledge existing theories, hypotheses, arguments and perspectives on your topic.

- Learn from experts and previous studies.

- Describe previous research methods and approaches.

- Uncover flaws in previous research.

- Outline gaps and missing information from previous research.

- Identify ways to expand, redefine or refocus discussions on your topic.

Sample Literature Review

Literature Review

Distance education and the progression of online learning are issues that are currently influencing higher education. Most of the research regarding distance education focuses on mainstream higher education institutions, but what about the historically black colleges and universities (HBCUs)? A few of these institutions across the country offer online courses, but the majority of them do not. How will these colleges continue to competitively educate 21st century students without solid distance education offerings? Will the digital divide affect the degree to which these institutions and its students participate in the landscape of higher education, which is constantly being impacted by the latest technologies?

Staff at the *Journal of Blacks in Higher Education* surveyed private and state HBCUs to determine the degree to which these colleges had adopted distance education programs. They reported that some of the top, nationally recognized HBCUs did not offer online courses. According to their findings, private HBCUs have been slow to embrace distance education, and that public black colleges and universities are far more likely than their private counterparts to have a presence in distance education (Distance Education, 2004). At the time of publication, Hampton University in Virginia had the most extensive distance education program. Since then, Howard University has joined the ranks as one of the more tech savvy HBCUs.

According to Smith (2011) *in HBCUs Must Embrace Online Education*, HBCUs are lagging behind the distance education trend, which compromises its competitiveness against other higher education institutions. Although many HBCU administrators perceive online learning as integral to their long-term goals, only 18 percent of these 105 active institutions offer online courses. In comparison, 66 percent of the nation's two- and four-year postsecondary institutions offer college-level distance education courses, according to the U.S. Department of Education.

The disparity between HBCUs and mainstream institutions in the area of distance education is significant. Currently, the University of Phoenix outpaces HBCUs in conferring more degrees to African American students. Smith argues that HBCUs can and should compete, and that these colleges should adopt aspects of the for-profit model when establishing distance education programs, so that they can continue to educate and produce leaders for the African American community.

Overcoming the Digital Divide

On the other hand, Stuart (2010) contends that many HBCUs are incapable of closing the digital divide. Stuart flatly states, "Closing the so-called digital divide is becoming less of a possibility for many HBCUs." He

cites lack of finances as a primary reason for HBCUs lack of adequate

technological infrastructure to support online learning or campus wide Wi-

Fi. Many HBCU campuses contain historic buildings, which are difficult

and costly to wire with modern computer technology. Morgan State

University is one of few HBCUs offering computer animation courses.

However, they must annually apply for grant funding to support this

and other technology initiatives, which is an unreliable source of revenue.

Even when HBCUs obtain equipment, many do not have the budget for

maintenance or the ability to sustain technology initiatives long term.

Although Smith believes HBCUs can develop competitive online programs,

Stuart argues that finances and infrastructure challenges prevent many of

these institutions from participating in the digital revolution at the same

pace and level as their mainstream counterparts.

Redd (2003) suggests that the digital divide persists at HBCUs,

because students have limited experience with computers before attending

college. She writes, "Even today, many students of color lack sufficient

exposure to computers because they come from low-income neighborhoods

with underfunded schools." What happens when these digitally deprived

students attend colleges and universities like HBCUs that cannot offer

sufficient access to computer technology? The long-term effect is that

African American students will graduate and enter the workforce unprepared for the requirements of above average technology skills in the workplace.

The general conclusion from the literature surveyed on HBCUs and distance education is that these schools must shore up their technology efforts in order to attract and enroll enough students to remain solvent and relevant in the landscape of 21st century higher education. In fact, this foreboding warning from the National Association for Equal Opportunity in its report titled *Historically Black colleges and universities: An assessment of networking and connectivity* still rings true:

> "During this era of continuous innovation and change, continual upgrading of networking and connectivity systems is critical if HBCUs are to continue to cross the digital divide and not fall victim to it. Failure to do this may result in what is a manageable digital divide today evolving into an unmanageable digital gulf tomorrow" (NAFEO, 2000).

References

Distance education is coming to the black colleges. (2004). *The Journal of Blacks in Higher Education,* (45), 112-112. Retrieved from http://search.proquest.com/docview/195540646?accountid=27965

National Association for Equal Opportunity. (2000). *Historically Black colleges and universities: An assessment of networking and connectivity.* Washington, DC: U.S. Department of Commerce, National Telecommunications Information Administration. Retrieved from http://search.ntia.doc.gov/nafeo.pdf.

Redd, Teresa M., (2003). "Tryin to make a dolla outa fifteen cent": Teaching composition with the internet at an HBCU. *Computers and Composition, 20*(4), 359-373. doi:10.1016/j.compcom.2003.08.012

Smith III, R. (2011). HBCUs Must Embrace Online Education. *Diverse: Issues in Higher Education, 28*(3), 25.

Stuart, R. (2010). Getting Connected. *Diverse: Issues in Higher Education, 27*(3), 13-14.

Theoretical Framework: African American learning styles and the academic achievement gap

Ashan R. Hampton

Anywhere University

Abstract

The achievement gap among African American students and other ethnicities has been a long source of perplexity, embarrassment and exasperation among American educators. Although much has been researched and written about the unique learning styles of African American students, their socioeconomic and intellectual challenges, little statistical progress has been demonstrated in closing this achievement gap.

In fact, African American students tend to drop out of high school in alarmingly disproportionate rates compared to other ethnic groups, particularly African American males. Considering the increasing need for educated citizens to meet the high technological demands of industry and daily living in a global, 21st century society, the low academic achievement of one ethnic group is simultaneously intriguing and problematic.

Keywords: achievement gap, social learning theory

Introduction

Unfortunately, the image of the Caucasian teacher's inability to effectively manage or engage minority students is cliché in the African American community. When listening to the frustrations of black parents whose children are not faring well in school, their exasperations boil down to the fact that they do not believe teachers of other ethnic groups can effectively teach their children – particularly, that white teachers exhibit the most difficulties in educating black children. Their opinions are not completely unfounded or merely the subjective rants of parents of low achieving students. Carter, Hawkins and Natesan note the historic difficulties the American educational system has experienced in properly educating African American students.

In their article titled, *The Relationship between Verve and the Academic Achievement of African American Students in Reading and Mathematics in an Urban Middle School* (2008), Carter, et. al write, "Its [the American public educational system] history of denial and discrimination in the education of Black children that has created a national crisis in which academic difficulty and school failure is disproportionately high" (p. 29). Despite all of the research, pedagogical workshops and curriculum reviews promulgated throughout the years in educational conferences and various professional meetings ad infinitum (and in some cases, ad nauseam), the education of African American students still suffers at the hands of uninformed instructors.

Why in the 21st century, with all kinds of educational technology available to school districts and individual teachers, is there such a gap between the academic progress of African American students and other ethnic groups in public education? It has been well documented that African American students experience extremely high dropout rates compared to their peers of other ethnicities. The Alliance for Excellent Education (2009) released a fact sheet on high school graduation rates that reported, "Nationally, about 71 percent of all students graduate from high school on time with a regular diploma, but barely half [50 percent] of African American and Hispanic students earn diplomas with their peers." These statistics empirically illuminate the current crisis African American students are facing in the public school system and validate the concerns, resentments and apathy African American parents feel toward public education and its employees, since they systematically fail to properly educate and prepare their children for 21st century living.

Learning Theory Information: Explaining the Achievement Gap

In their struggles to identify concrete reasons for the pervasive academic deficiencies demonstrated by African American students, some researchers have turned to examinations of socioeconomic influences for answers. In *Class and categories: What role does socioeconomic status play in children's lexical and conceptual development?* J. Bloomquist (2009) posits that deficient or delayed language use and the resulting compromised ability to read at grade level pose linguistic and academic challenges in the classroom for both teachers and students. Bloomquist cites differences in social class and how working-class parents relay linguistic information to children in early childhood compared to middle class parents.

Conclusion

African American students are negatively impacted by a systematic neglect of their unique learning styles and needs on behalf of teachers, educational policy makers and other school officials. Although several possible causes of the achievement gap among African American students have been briefly explored in this paper and extensively researched across professional and academic disciplines, the result of the educational crisis experienced by this demographic produces extensive and devastating consequences for society at large.

In sum, when students are not effectively instructed in the classroom, for whatever reasons, their motivation to learn and confidence in their academic abilities decrease, especially since many of them are referred to disability services when they behave in accordance to their cultural influences and practices.

References

Alliance for Excellent Education. (2009). *High School Drop outs in America* [Fact sheet]. Washington, D. C.: Author.

Associated Press (2009). Black-white student achievement gap persists. Retrieved from MSNBC.com

http://www.msnbc.msn.com/id/31911075/ns/us_news-education

Bloomquist, J. (2009). Class and categories: What role does socioeconomic status play in children's lexical and conceptual development? *Multilingua, 28*(4), 327-353. doi:10.1515/mult.2009.015.

Carter, N., Hawkins, T., & Natesan, P. (2008). The Relationship between Verve and the Academic Achievement of African American Students in Reading and Mathematics in an Urban Middle School. *Educational Foundations*, 22(1-2), 29-46. Retrieved from ERIC database.

More Resources from
Ashan R. Hampton

B & W Print
ISBN: 978-1-387-91413-5

Grammar Essentials for Proofreading, Copyediting & Business Writing focuses on the grammar and usage topics you need to improve your writing skills for personal and professional success. Learn how to correct common grammar errors like fragments, run-ons, and comma splices while answering usage concerns such as when to use "who" or "whom." Each chapter ends with practical, self-grading exercises.

Ordering information:

www.arhampton.com/books
www.lulu.com

B & W Print
ISBN: 978-1-678-15094-5

"Creative Business Writing" teaches uncreative people how to use expository writing skills to produce descriptive workplace documents. Readers will build confidence in developing informative and engaging business documents by using a variety of expository writing techniques.

Ordering information:

www.arhampton.com/books
www.lulu.com

More Writing Resources

Have you been out of the classroom for a while? Learn to effectively correct common grammar errors. **Adult Learner Grammar Essentials** teaches you to effectively correct the most common grammar errors encountered in academic and professional writing. With self-study quizzes, plain English explanations and real-world examples, you will improve your grammar skills in just minutes a day.

ISBN: 978-035-969282-8

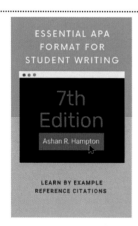

Essential APA Format for Student Writing provides examples of reference citations and samples of student papers. Instead of slogging through the entire APA manual or fumbling around on the internet to find examples, student writers can use this book as a quick reference guide on how to write and arrange APA research papers. In addition to general APA guidelines, this book offers learn-by-example guidance on the fundamentals of APA.

ISBN: 978-1-716-73759-6

Can you catch mistakes in your own writing? Can you identify and correct common writing errors? Would you like to become an effective proofreader for personal growth or profit? **Proofreading Power: Skills & Drills** provides essential rules, guidelines and tips to quickly boost your editing prowess. Train your eye to catch mistakes in the smallest of details with practical exercises on grammar, mechanics, usage, and spelling.

ISBN: 978-1-387-95472-8

www.arhampton.com/books

References

American Psychological Association. *Style and Grammar Guidelines*. APA Style. https://apastyle.apa.org/style-grammar-guidelines.

Capella University. *Basic Steps in the Research Process*. Library Research and Information Literacy Skills. https://www.nhcc.edu/student-resources/library/doinglibraryresearch/basic-steps-in-the-research-process.

Capella University. *Get Critical Search Skills*. Library Research and Information Literacy Skills. https://campus.capella.edu/library/library-research-skills/searching-effectively.

Capella University. *Think Critically About Source Quality*. Library Research and Information Literacy Skills. https://campus.capella.edu/library/library-research-skills/evaluating-source-quality.

Capella University. *What is Scholarly?* Library Research and Information Literacy Skills. https://campus.capella.edu/library/library-research-skills/identifying-scholarly-resources/what-is-scholarly.

Harris, R. (2018, October 11). *Evaluating Internet Research Sources*. https://www.virtualsalt.com/evalu8it.htm.

Hartness Library. *What are Peer-Reviewed Journals?* Peer-Reviewed Articles. https://hartness.vsc.edu/find/articles/peer-reviewed.

Humboldt State University (n.d.). *Search Strategy Worksheet* http://library.wcsu.edu/people/tom/SearchStrategyWorksheet_WRT101.pdf

Lloyd Sealy Library. *What Is Peer Review?* Evaluating Information Sources. https://guides.lib.jjay.cuny.edu/c.php?g=288333.

SDSU Library. *What is a scholarly journal?* Peer-Reviewed Articles. https://library.sdsu.edu/research-services/research-help/peer-reviewed-articles.

Smith, S. (2020, April 28). *Critical writing*. https://www.eapfoundation.com/writing/critical.

Wagenmakers, E.-J. (2009, April 1). *Teaching Graduate Students How to Write Clearly*. https://www.psychologicalscience.org/observer/teaching-graduate-students-how-to-write-clearly.

Index

Made in the USA
Columbia, SC
18 May 2022

60609270R00086